T0017345

JANET MELROSE &
SHERYL NORMANDEAU

The Prairie Gardener's Go-To for
Fruit

TOUCHWOOD

TouchWood Editions
touchwoodeditions.com

The information in this book is true and complete to the best of the authors' knowledge. All recommendations are made without guarantee on the part of the authors or the publisher.

Copy edited by Warren Layberry

Proofread by Meg Yamamoto

Designed by Tree Abraham

Photos by Janet Melrose and Sheryl Normandeau with the following exceptions: p. 49 (Ahmet Yasti / shutterstock.com), p. 93 (courtesy of Tina Boisvert), p. 77 (IanRedding / shutterstock.com), p. 101 (aleori / shutterstock.com).

CATALOGUING DATA AVAILABLE FROM LIBRARY AND ARCHIVES CANADA

ISBN 9781771513906 (print)

ISBN 9781771513913 (electronic)

TouchWood Editions acknowledges that the land on which we live and work is within the traditional territories of the Lkwungen (Esquimalt and Songhees), Malahat, Pacheedaht, Scia'new, T'sou-ke, wsáneć (Pauquachin, Tsartlip, Tsawout, Tseycum) peoples.

We acknowledge the financial support of the Government of Canada through the Canada Book Fund, and the province of British Columbia through the Book Publishing Tax Credit.

This book was produced using FSC®-certified, acid-free papers, processed chlorine free, and printed with soya-based inks.

Printed in China

27 26 25 24 23 1 2 3 4 5

Dedicated to all prairie gardeners

Introduction

Growing food is a huge deal for us—and for so many of the gardeners we chat with. Many of us are gardening to help feed our families and friends, which might reduce the rising cost of the grocery bill. Then there is also the unparalleled taste of produce fresh from the garden to consider! Other gardeners are interested in growing plants that have it all: ornamental appeal *and* delicious food. (It's hard not to when we see and smell the breathtaking flowers of an apple or cherry tree in the spring and then excitedly realize we can harvest fruit from them later in the season!) We're thrilled at the prospect of harvesting fruit for eating out of hand, for baking, and for making preserves. We want to share the bounty of our crabapple or raspberry harvest with others. We wish to construct hedges or windbreaks composed of fruit trees or set up a multi-storeyed food forest. Whether we are growing an orchard in a rural area, planting a couple of currant bushes or haskaps in a small urban yard, or growing squash on a balcony, we are interested in the beauty, the potential for wildlife habitat, and the seriously yummy eats that result from growing fruit plants.

It's primarily about the fruit, of course, but the annual spring display of many fruit plants is one of the other reasons we love them.

In *The Prairie Gardener's Go-To for Fruit*, we want to further your success in gardening with edible plants! Whether you are an experienced gardener, new to the whole gig, or somewhere in between, we want to help you plan, plant, and care for your fruit plants and deal with any problems that may arise. We also want to give you some guidance to properly harvest and store your bounty. We tackle important topics such as mulching, fertilizing, watering, pruning, and propagation. We give you the lowdown on some pests and diseases that may affect your plants, and we offer some answers to specific questions about growing fruit crops. Let's explore these fun and rewarding plants!—SHERYL NORMANDEAU & JANET MELROSE

What is the botanical definition of a fruit?

We all know what a "fruit" is. It is that sweet and crisp apple or peach with juice dripping down your arm. It's the sun-warmed raspberry you pop in your mouth or tart sour cherry on a loaded tree. Robins, bears, and squirrels, not to mention people, adore fruit.

It's not that simple though, as the term "fruit" is loaded with botanical, culinary, and even legal meanings, some of which are fun trivia, but others might impact the tax you pay. Some extra botanical knowledge will deepen your awe for the plant kingdom and how it has co-evolved with other kingdoms. Not only that, such knowledge will help you be a successful and satisfied fruit gardener, especially when you are enjoying that strawberry you grew and got to harvest before anyone else!

Botanically, a fruit is a "mature ovary, along with its associated parts."[1] Another way of describing a fruit is as an "edible reproductive body of a plant."[2] But what

does all that really encompass exactly? In layman's terms, a fruit is literally the end result of a plant flowering and being fertilized through its carpels receiving viable pollen, should we gardeners not snip off the blooms as they fade. Changes occur in a fertilized flower—with anthers and stamens withering away, petals dropping, and sepals either following or morphing for further use. The ovary within the flower enlarges with cell walls multiplying, expanding, and thickening as the ovules start to develop seed within; this ripened ovary is known as the *pericarp*. In some species, as the fruit nears maturity, the hormone ethylene is released and the flesh of the fruit sweetens and softens. When mature, the fruit either remains on the plant, dehydrating until such time as the mature seeds are released, or the entire fruit drops to the soil to eventually germinate where it lands after the pericarp degrades, assuming of course that no one eats it first.

Botanically, then, fruits are squash, legume pods, tomatoes, peppers, apples, pears, berries, nuts, and a plethora of others we may or may not think of as fruit. Hence the debate as to whether a tomato is a fruit or vegetable because, culturally and especially in our cuisine, we make the determination between vegetable and fruit as whether it is savory or sweet. An okra is not sweet at all, so it is a vegetable. But no one thinks of an apple as anything but a fruit. We even make the determination between fruit and vegetable based on whether it is a dessert or part of the main course. Or whether it is eaten raw or cooked, though that one is easily debunked considering what we use to make salads these days. Yet the culinary definition of a vegetable is any part of a plant that is not the botanical fruit. We eat only the stalk of a rhubarb, so it is really a vegetable. But rhubarb gets to be a fruit because we enjoy it either dipped in sugar and eaten raw or cooked in sweet pies and cobblers. Thus, avocados are treated as vegetables because they go into salads, in guacamole, or on toast. No one particularly uses tomatoes as a dessert, though there is tomato soup cake to belie that assumption. Some common spices are also fruits. Think of the vanilla bean, not to mention paprika made from red peppers. Some nuts are actually fruits and vice versa. The debate goes on and on to lots of laughter and we learn as we delve deeper into botany.

Legally it gets rather interesting, yet still amusing, when you consider that, back in 1893, the United States Supreme Court made the determination that a tomato is a vegetable simply to ensure that tomatoes paid a 10 percent import tariff rather than none at all if they were deemed to be fruit.[3] **—JM**

Journalist and humorist Miles Kington philosophically mused: "Knowledge is knowing that a tomato is a fruit; wisdom is not putting it in a fruit salad."[4] (We won't mention the ingredients lists of certain salsas, then!)

Peppers are also considered fruit.

Plant Selection
and Planning

What are some of the different types of fleshy fruit?

Botanically, fruits are divided between those that are dry dehiscent (opening to discharge seeds) or indehiscent (not opening to discharge seeds) and those with fleshy, fibrous, or even stony tissue enclosed in a relatively soft skin or pericarp.

Fruit classification is further divided as to how many carpels comprise the fruit—usually one or two, but sometimes many. To complicate life further, it matters too whether the floral tube, stem axis, or other parts are present within the fruit.

We typically lump all those that are dry into the unscientific category of "seed heads" as the pericarp that surrounds the seeds within dries as the seeds mature, only to split open to release their bounty to the wind, water, and coats of animals.

Fleshy fruits are those with that, well, fleshy tissue that is often succulent, sweet, or otherwise desirable to us and the rest of the animal world. I can well believe that plants evolved fleshy fruits to attract animals to consume them, scarifying the seeds within as they travel through the bodies of said animals to be finally expelled far from home. Ingenious, I call it, not to mention fun and nutritious for the animal.

We further divide fleshy fruits into categories as to how many carpels comprise them and the structure of the pericarp. The endocarp is the innermost layer, usually enclosing the seeds. The mesocarp is the flesh of the fruit, while the epicarp is the skin, be it thin and easy to break or hard and thick.

Those that are "drupes" form from a single carpel, have a stony endocarp—most often with just a single seed within—and soft flesh and thin skins. Think plum, cherry, peach, and olive, but also dates, pecans, and macadamia. A coconut is a dry drupe, because it has that leathery skin, as are walnuts and butternuts. But not avocados!

"Berries," on the other hand, have fleshy endocarps and mesocarps and either the thinnest of epicarps or rather tough alternatives. They can be formed from just the one carpel and hence one seed, as with nutmeg and—you guessed

Winter squash is botanically a fruit—specifically, a pepo.

it—the avocado. They can have many seeds that are enclosed, as with grapes, gooseberries, currants, saskatoons, goji berry, tomatoes, papaya, and guava, but not strawberries or raspberries. The pomegranate isn't a "pome," despite its name, but a berry where the aril around each seed is what we consume. The banana is sometimes included as being a parthenocarpic berry because it develops even without pollination or fertilization, though some consider it a "pepo" because of its skin. By the way, the fruit of a potato is a berry!

Think of a pepo as a berry with a rind for an epicarp, either soft like the banana or cucumber or hard like most of the winter squashes.

Citrus fruits are "hesperidia," berries whose epicarp is a leathery rind, but also with membranes between each section.

Pity the poor blueberry, which is an *inferior* berry because it develops from an "inferior" ovary and parts of the flower are incorporated into the fruit.

Then there is a whole other section of fleshy fruits—those with one or more carpels but with floral tubes or stem axes being an integral part of the fruit. "Pomes" are those fruits with stony or cartilaginous endocarps enclosing the seeds, along with fleshy mesocarps and thin epicarps. Think of those bits that get stuck in our teeth if we bite into the core of an apple. Many species in the rose family (Rosaceae) are pomes, such as pears, mountain ash berries, and quinces.

Strawberries, raspberries, and rosehips are "aggregate" fruit, either dry "achenes" on the inside or outside of a fleshy receptacle or a collection of "drupelets." Guess which one is which!

Lastly, there are multiple fruits formed from many flowers fused together to form one fruit with the pineapple being the best example.

Many people think of a fruit as an apple, banana, blueberry, or orange. But gardeners think of fruit as drupes, pomes, berries, and pepos, and a whole new world opens up for us![1] —JM

Rosehips are aggregate fruits. (Now, what's an achene again? It's the membrane that surrounds each seed inside the hip.)

Do all fruit plants need full sun, or can some handle shadier spots?

It can't be denied that our apples, pears, cherries, plums, and apricots need all the sun they can get in our northern latitudes to mature fruit before fall frosts come. The average requirement for fruit trees is between six and eight hours of direct sunlight to maximize photosynthesis. Flower and fruit development takes a lot of energy. Fruits grown in full sun are often sweeter. However, too much sun can also be detrimental as maturing fruits are subject to sunburn from too much direct light and heat.

Some large fruit trees can handle less sunlight and still produce well. In 2021, some pear trees I had the joy of harvesting were loaded down, and they receive only westerly sun in the afternoon, after being totally in shade until after two o'clock. Sour cherries are perfectly happy with six hours or less. Some plum varieties are also able to do well in partial shade for part of the day.

However, the general rule that the more sun the better is true for these large fruit species. Even just a few extra hours in shade will affect productivity both in the size of their fruit and in numbers. Being in shade may also affect their ability to withstand winter stresses and may encourage pests.

It's a different matter for small fruit-bearing shrubs. Dappled shade, morning sun with afternoon shade, and even filtered, indirect light can be just the ticket for many species. Saskatoons, blueberries, haskaps, elderberries, gooseberries, and currants are all good producers in dappled shade. Rhubarb prefers sun, but in partial shade the flavour is sweeter. I find that, too, with my raspberries that somehow ended up growing underneath a pin cherry tree. There is less fruit, but man oh man, they are sweet and succulent, and I never worry about them desiccating in hot sun.

Strawberries, on the other hand, do need that full sun, except for alpine strawberries which flourish in partial shade.

There are certain considerations to keep in mind when growing fruit in partial shade. The soil tends to stay frozen longer in spring, delaying flowering, which is sometimes a good thing given the prairies' propensity for that last killer frost after we think we are safe. Likewise, if you can site them on a slope, the cold air from unseasonably cool spells will have a chance to drain away and cause less damage. In shade, the soil remains wetter for longer, so monitor to ensure the soil has a chance to dry out before watering again. Amend the soil so that it is well draining. Space out the plants farther than you might to ensure good air circulation so foliage doesn't stay damp after rains. This practice also helps reduce humidity so fungal spores don't have the opportunity to stay on foliage long enough to infect the leaves. If the shade is too dense and it is possible to do so, prune out some branches of trees overhead to allow more light. There is not much we can do about buildings, so if the shade they cast is too dense for too long, you may have to relocate some species to more favourable localities.

We really don't have to forgo our fruit if our gardens are shadier than not. We may not be able to grow apples, but there are lots of other choices to compensate![2] —JM

Give your strawberries plenty of sun if you want top-notch fruit production.

Is it better to buy bare-root fruit plants, or those grown in a container?

There are significant advantages and disadvantages for both bare-root and container fruit plants, including selection, cost, ease of transplanting, and ease of the plant settling into its new home.

Bare-root fruit and other plants are available only in spring when they are still in a dormant state. They must be transplanted right away as they come out of dormancy quickly. Generally, they are young specimens and if planted carefully will have little to no transplant shock.

There is a greater selection of varieties with bare-root fruit plants as you can source from nurseries that specialize in fruit species. They cost less because the time invested by the nurseryman is less given that they are usually either whips (only a year old) or saplings (two to three years old), and there isn't the cost of container and soil. There is usually a greater root mass ratio as the methods to harvest them are minimally injurious. It is easier to train a bare-root plant as you are almost rearing it from infancy.

That said, when buying bare-root plants, there may be a requirement for a minimum number to order. No problem if you are establishing a mini-orchard or food forest, or have a large garden, but if you need only one or two, you may not be able to find a place that will ship to you. It is seldom that a reseller of plants will carry bare-root fruit trees and shrubs.

A downside is the time it will take for the plant to mature enough to bear fruit. There is a lot of growing that will need to be done before they have the energy to devote to flowering and maturing fruit.

Plants grown in containers flip those considerations. They are usually older plants, and many will bear fruit the same season that they are planted. They are available for most of the growing season, often into fall when it is a good time to plant them. The selection is not as extensive, as garden centres and nurseries must look to what is most popular as well as available. However, there is no minimum number to be purchased, which is ideal for a gardener wanting only a few, but of different species or cultivars. Their cost is greater, reflecting the time and training that is needed to grow them to fair-sized saplings and older specimens.

Because the specimens are older and may have been living in their container for a year or more, there is significantly more top structure than roots to support them, and the chance of them being root bound increases the larger the plant. Transplant shock is more of a concern, given the handling they need to be planted correctly, and they will take longer to establish. Those already in flower—or even maturing fruit—may lose that crop after planting as the plant prioritizes root growth over propagation. It is even recommended that you nip off flowers and fruit after planting to reduce the energy demands on it as it settles into its new home. The bonus is that, next season, you are likely to have fruit on a plant that is large enough to be a significant feature in the garden right away.

There is no absolute best choice between bare-root and container plants, and in the end it all comes down to what is best for the gardener and their garden.[3]—JM

While container-grown trees may have ample top growth, their roots may be small and restricted.

Are all fruit plants self-fertile? Which common ones need pollinizer plants to help them cross-pollinate?

It is a real mixed bag out there of species that are self-pollinators and those that require cross-pollination. Plus, there are ones that are self-pollinators but produce much more fruit if cross-pollination occurs.

While pollination is simply the transfer of pollen from the anther on stamens (male part) to the stigma on the pistil (female part), it is not so simple as all that. Species that are self-fertile or self-fruitful can be successfully pollinated by pollen from flowers on the same tree or shrub, sometimes even from the same flower if the bee or other pollinator visits it multiple times. Those that are self-unfruitful require cross-pollination, where pollen from another genetically different variety or species is required for fertilization and fruit set to occur. Even though the flowers are perfect (containing both male and female parts) they are genetically incompatible so they cannot fertilize themselves. This ensures genetic diversity of the species. A few species do have male and female plants and are generally sold with tags indicating the sex of the plant. Arctic kiwi and sea buckthorn are two such species. Likewise, many of our perfect flowering varieties and cultivars have wild species with male and female plants. They only bear perfect flowers due to breeding efforts to create fruit trees and shrubs that work in smaller garden spaces.[4]

While bees and other pollinators travel a fair distance at times, do not rely on neighbouring trees and shrubs to be cross-pollinators. It is recommended that a suitable variety be planted within fifty feet (fifteen metres) to ensure good cross-pollination. Techniques of close planting, whereby trees or shrubs are planted approximately eighteen inches (forty-five centimetres) apart and then trained either to grow away from each other or as hedges, can reduce the footprint that multiple varieties of the same species would normally occupy and take care of pollination to boot. Close planting requires annual training to ensure good air circulation, non-competing branches, and attention to their nutrient needs, but it can be rewarding.[5] Alternatively, choosing multi-grafted trees can make sense.

The most reliably self-fruitful species happen to be our berries. Strawberries, raspberries, and grapes are all reliably self pollinating species. Mind you, who has just one strawberry plant, raspberry bush, or grapevine? Saskatoons, too, are reliably self-fruitful, as are sour cherries.

Blueberries are considered self-fruitful, but having two or three different varieties will boost production considerably, and if varieties with differing maturity periods are chosen, it will extend the bounty. The same is true for currants, gooseberries, and highbush cranberries.

Haskaps (also known as sweet honeysuckle or honeyberry) absolutely require cross-pollination, and not just any old variety with another. There are specific groups of cultivars that will pollinate each other. Mixing in a cultivar from another group may not give reliable pollination. For example, mid-season 'Tundra', 'Borealis', 'Aurora', and 'Honey Bee' pollinate each other but not late-ripening cultivars 'Boreal Blizzard' or 'Boreal Beauty', which require 'Boreal Beast' as their pollinator. The older Russian cultivars 'Cinderella', 'Polar Jewel', and 'Berry Blue' used to be considered good pollinators for other groups, but their berries are smaller and tarter.[6] It gets complicated, and for success, you need to research the selections before buying.

Large fruit species are generally self-unfruitful. Apples must always have two distinct varieties to be fruitful. Pears are considered self-unfruitful, though there tends to be some disagreement, and it really does depend on the variety. Having two or more varieties does boost production though. The same is also true for plums and apricots. Sometimes cherry and pin cherry are posited as suitable cross-pollinators, as they are all in the *Prunus* genus, but it comes down to bloom times matching.

The net result is that if you can—even for self-fruitful species—have more than one plant, you will invariably have better pollination and fruit set occurring and, fingers crossed, bountiful harvests.[7]—JM

Haskaps have very specific needs when it comes to pollinizers.

Can I grow strawberries and other small fruit plants in raised beds? Will the plants survive the winter?

It is entirely possible—and in some instances preferable—to have small fruits growing in raised beds. Large fruits that typically grow as trees are not so well suited to raised beds due to their greater space requirements, not to mention big root systems, unless it is a very large raised bed.

But our strawberries, blueberries, currants, gooseberries, haskaps, goji berries, and even raspberries are well suited to raised beds, low or tall.

Raised beds allow us to tailor the soil to match the needs of various species, especially pH, nutrient levels, and moisture retention capacity. It is easy to provide mulch to conserve soil moisture and reduce weed seeds blowing in. Most fruit species do not compete well with perennial weeds, so the ability to deter (prevent?) those tough-to-remove rhizomatous roots is a real bonus. On the flip side, those fruit species with wandering roots, and I am thinking raspberries here, or those that love to create thickets, such as goji berries, are thoroughly contained within a raised bed if it is tall enough. It is also easier to protect crops from birds and other fruit-snacking animals.

Yes, you can grow strawberries in raised beds!

From the harvesting perspective, it is a breeze as bending over to get those low-down berries is much reduced.

The concern, as ever, is winter damage to roots with the cold being able to penetrate through the sides of the raised beds. Thus, the key to success is choosing the hardiest species and cultivars in the first place. A garden I regularly visit has grown haskaps, raspberries, and strawberries in metal raised beds for six years now and has not lost a one. Proof positive, as far as I am concerned, for those species. Our native species of currants, gooseberries, and blueberries—all hardy to zone 2—are also good candidates.

Do ensure that the raised bed is large enough to provide a goodly soil mass to accommodate substantial root systems. A large volume of soil will not flash-freeze, either, the first time our temperatures do a deep dive. Smaller raised beds may benefit from being insulated with straw around the sides if that is possible.

Otherwise, just go for it. Success will be yours![8]—JM

How do I encourage pollinators such as bees to my fruit plants?

Fruit trees and shrubs, by and large, are pollinated by insects. But not just bees, native or otherwise. Wasps, flies, beetles, ants, butterflies, and moths are part of the picture too.

To encourage ever more pollinators to be in the garden and busily visiting every flower on your fruit plants, it is essential to provide the habitat that they need.

Many orchardists, these days, are underplanting their trees with flowering plants that will provide a full season's worth of pollen and nectar. Not ones that flower at the same time as the trees and shrubs above, but earlier and later in the season. Spring-flowering bulbs along with ubiquitous dandelions are the first to have a heavy nectar load at an important time when insects are emerging. Skip species that flower in May into early June, but load up with species that typically flower from July onwards, and don't forget the late bloomers of fall. Most pollinators are generalists, able and willing to visit a multitude of different shapes of flowers. But they appreciate a biodiverse garden with something for everyone, meaning shrubs, herbaceous perennials and flowering annuals and vegetables. What most pollinators do not care for are substantially altered hybrid plants whose pollen centres are hard to reach or altogether inaccessible—or those hybrids that are sterile.

Do provide access to moisture. A very shallow dish of water with rocks to rest on will attract many a bee, wasp, and fly, while a damp patch of soil will be perfect for butterflies by day and moths by night. It is imperative that any water source provided is not deep as insects easily drown if their wings get wet.

Insects are no different from us. They require shelter from adverse weather. A wild area in the garden with a mess of twigs and branches, grasses, old logs, and a thick layer of decaying leaves is just the ticket to weather out rain, heat, and wind. Planting in layers with different levels of canopy is excellent—include species of differing heights and sizes. The idea is to have a niche for everyone to shelter.

Just as importantly, nesting sites along with larval hosts will encourage pollinators to really make their homes in the garden. They don't need to be elaborate—though we do love to build nesting boxes. Old logs or still-standing trees are prime habitat. A simple patch of bare soil allows access for burrowing life. That wild area too will provide suitable habitat for larvae to pupate. It is even better if the sites are not fully exposed to wind, rain, or hot sun. Leave perennials standing in winter, especially those with hollow stems. We don't like rain beating in our doors and windows and neither do pollinators.

Paramount is the need to minimize — or better yet eliminate altogether — the use of pesticides within the garden, and that includes any DIY pesticides too. Most pesticides are not specific to one species, and the harm they can do to the innocent outweighs, in many instances, the measure of control they provide for pests. The principles of Integrated Pest Management (IPM) include accepting the rough with the smooth to a greater or lesser extent as we strive to create a balanced and healthy environment that will be the most welcoming to pollinators as well as all comers.

We know we are successful when we enjoy a truly noisy garden with many insects, birds, and small mammals going about their business among laden fruit trees and shrubs.[9]—JM

Calendula is a colourful annual that can be underplanted with fruit trees and shrubs to encourage bees and other pollinators to visit.

Care and Maintenance

2

Should I mulch my fruit plants? If so, what are the best mulches to use and how much should I add?

Absolutely, we should be mulching under all our fruit trees and shrubs, bar none. We discussed the benefits of mulching extensively in *The Prairie Gardener's Go-To for Soil*, but to briefly underline the benefits of mulch, consider that it conserves moisture in the soil, moderates the soil temperature in both hot and cold spells, suppresses weeds, reduces splashback, which carries pathogens to the leaves of our plants, and, best of all, contributes to soil improvement generally and soil biology in particular.

Seeing as most of our fruit-bearing plants are woody, they benefit from a mulch that is woody too. Wood chips (not fresh), post peelings, fallen leaves, and leaf mulch are all excellent mulches for the purpose. As they degrade into the soil, they will contribute to the fungally dominated soil that trees and shrubs prefer and foster the natural fertility system that cycles materials such as leaves shed by trees each fall back into the soil.

Strawberries should be mulched with straw because how else can they be called strawberries? More importantly, herbaceous plants prefer a more bacterially dominated soil, and the carbon that straw contributes to the soil as it breaks down greatly assists in creating the optimum soil biology. The straw lifts the berries off the soil surface, reducing potential for botrytis and other pathogens spoiling the fruit. However, nothing is amiss with other mulches such as dry grass clippings and fallen leaves. Any mulch works so long as it doesn't compact easily and sheds moisture readily, keeping the berries nice and dry as they ripen.

Woody mulches should be evenly applied as a layer to the drip line, no deeper than four inches (ten centimetres), and not piled up against the trunk like a volcano, which creates a host of problems. If there is concern about potential for nitrogen inhibition, spread a thin layer of alfalfa pellets—they are high in nitrogen—to counteract the possibility. Softer materials such as fallen leaves, leaf mulch, grass clippings, and straw can be applied in greater amounts, up to eight inches (twenty centimetres), as they will readily shrink down.

Rodents, such as voles, taking up residence in mulch is often cited as a concern, though a couple of cats hanging around will take care of that possibility. Cats aside, do ensure that the mulches are pulled back from the crowns and trunks of plants to avoid creating easy access to the bark in winter.

Mulches should be replenished periodically as they degrade into the soil, with woody mulches typically lasting much longer than straw, leaves, and grass clippings.[1] —JM

These strawberry plants are nestled into a mulch of straw.

Does hilling strawberries result in larger berries? If so, how do I go about doing it?

Hilling strawberries is more a planting system and technique rather than planting in beds that are mounded. It certainly is not the same as hilling potatoes, which involves mounding soil around the stems to promote more potato tubers. Doing that would swiftly kill strawberry plants!

Rather, the name comes about because the strawberry plants look like little hills in the bed in which they are growing. You can employ this planting system in flat-to-the-ground, mounded, or raised beds, even large containers. It works equally well for all. The goal is to boost strawberry production overall by driving the plants' energy toward developing fruit on the mother plant rather than toward propagating through runners.

The planting method involves creating three rows that are spaced twelve to fifteen inches apart (thirty to thirty-eight centimetres). Then space the plants within the rows the same amount but stagger them so that the middle row is offset by six to eight inches (fifteen to twenty centimetres) to provide maximum leaf canopy and growing space. If you want further rows, then have a walking space of one and a half to two feet (forty-five to sixty centimetres) between each set of three rows for ease of access.

Hilling can promote better strawberry fruit production — and who doesn't want that?

The technique part comes in when the plants start to produce runners. Allow the runners to develop two to three leaves as they start to root, but then, just before the new daughter plant has a chance to firmly root, snip off the runners. Cutting the runners before this stage will promote further runners growing, diverting more energy into runner production. With the runners removed the mother plant then devotes its energy to developing into larger plants along with flowering and producing a bigger crop, though not necessarily bigger fruit. As an aside, the first flower on any stem will be the biggest and the others will be smaller. Keep checking every few weeks to make sure that the mother plant has got the message.

Do select varieties and cultivars that naturally produce fewer runners. Day-neutral cultivars are the best choices for this system. Although it can work with June-bearing cultivars as well, there will be more runner snipping required. Everbearing strawberries will just keep on wanting to send out more and more runners.

Choosing a raised bed or mounded bed over in ground will assist with ensuring that water doesn't pool around the plants and lead to rot. Besides, the plants will really look like hills then![2] —JM

What are the best practices for watering my fruit plants while they are actively growing? What about withholding water just before the plants bear fruit? I've heard that is a good idea.

We have all, at some point, bitten into a fruit and found it to contain too much moisture and little taste. Cherries and other soft fruit split, turn to mush, and develop moulds. Apples, pears, and other large fruit ripen prematurely and have little taste.

Most often the quality of our fruits' taste, texture, appearance, and nutrient density is down to natural weather events, such as a rainy early summer, and there is little we can do about that. But we can ensure that our own cultural practices are spot-on, and we can change them up to accommodate, and even mitigate, how climate and seasonal weather will affect plants and the fruit they produce in any given season.

The foundation, as always, is the soil. Fruit species are no exception to the general rule that moisture-retentive but well-draining soils are best for plant health. There are exceptions, of course, based on the natural habitat of any species, ranging from bog cranberry (*Vaccinium oxycoccos*) to prickly pear (*Opuntia* spp.), which require specific soil conditions. Generally, however, both parched soil and saturated soil lead to numerous conditions that affect the health of the plant and its ability to produce fruit. Waterlogged soil will result in premature drop of flowers and fruit. Plants that experience dry soils to the point that they wilt will incur root damage, leaves withering, and fruit drop.

The best cultural watering practices ensure that the soil is consistently moist, but not wet. Deep watering is encouraged, such that when applying water, it has a chance to sink through the entire soil profile to a depth of two feet (sixty centimetres). A moisture meter meant for the outdoors is a handy tool to use to gauge when to water. Do not wait until you observe wilting. Young plants, with their small root masses, require the most attention to ensure that they receive adequate water, but as the plants establish, that vigilance can be relaxed except in periods of high heat and drought. A regular routine to check soil moisture and apply water as necessary—rather than watering to a set schedule—will go a long way to ensuring that our fruiting species are able to access the moisture they need when they need it.

The periods that fruiting species require the most water for their needs is after leaf out, around flowering, and up to harvest time. Once the fruit has been harvested, the plants are not growing as much, and if the harvest period is in early fall, the plant will be entering into a period of dormancy and preparing for winter.

Specifically withholding water when fruit is maturing is not necessary, as the plants themselves have got it all figured out. Our role is to provide optimum soil and growing conditions, as much as we can within reason, and choose the best species for those conditions. Plus, of course, appreciate the fruit they do mature in any given season, considering everything that goes into growing it.[3] —JM

Watering carefully and regularly is critical to plant health.

What types of fertilizer or amendment should I use for my fruit plants? Is there an optimum time to apply it?

If you are establishing new garden beds or a site for your orchard, do a soil test first to determine if there are any nutrient deficiencies. If a soil test indicates that amendments are necessary, add them at the recommended rate. If your soil test indicates that nitrogen is deficient, you can try applications of organic amendments such as alfalfa meal, blood meal, or fish meal. Bone meal can supply some phosphorus, if needed, and greensand can help if potassium is lacking. There is no need to add any of these if they're not needed—don't waste your money or resources. In the case of nitrogen, too much may cause your plants to suffer insofar as flower and fruit production goes.

When planting your fruit plants, there is no need to add fertilizer or amendments to the planting hole; your soil should already be in good condition and ready to accept the plants you've selected.

For established fruit plants, add a two-inch (five-centimetre) layer of compost as a side dressing each spring. There is no need to dig in the amendment; watering will help the nutrients move into the soil so that the plants can take them up.[4]—sn

Weeding = healthier fruit plants. Why? Let us tell you!

Weeds and even the seemingly innocent turfgrass that makes up your lawn can be huge competitors of fruit plants for sunlight, nutrients, water, and space. If you want your fruit plants to thrive, the encroaching plants must go! Herbicides can damage the fruit plant through spray drift or translocation through the soil, so avoid the chemicals and stick to good old elbow grease instead. It may be hard work, tedious, and repetitive, but weeding by pulling up the unwanted plants by hand is the safest for your cultivated plants. If you are tempted to get a digging tool in there close to your fruit plants, be extremely careful as it could result in possible root damage.—SN

Should I stake my newly planted fruit trees?

It's a good idea to do so! Stake your young fruit trees for up to two years after planting, especially if you live in an extremely windy area. Most grafted fruit trees on dwarfing rootstocks should be staked for life; their root systems don't always provide the support that they need to stay sturdy and upright, so staking gives them a needed leg-up.

The two-stake method is a quick, easy way to stake your trees:

Select two wooden or metal stakes that are taller than the young tree you have planted. You want to be able to drive the stakes into the ground between one and two feet (thirty to sixty centimetres) for stability, so measure accordingly.

Drive the stakes into place, on opposite sides of the tree. Each stake should be positioned about twelve inches (thirty centimetres) from the trunk.

Wrap soft ties around the tree and affix it to the stakes. You can buy kits of soft rubber hose and ties in your garden centre. Loosen the ties as the tree grows in girth. You don't want to girdle the tree with a constrictive tie.[5] —SN

Should I trellis my raspberries, hardy kiwi plants, squash, and hops? What are some good ways to do this?

Fruit that grows via canes or on vines really benefits from being on trellises. Not only is a trellis an attractive feature that presents the fruit beautifully, but it also makes the fruit infinitely more accessible for harvesting.

Ever gotten scratches or been tripped up by canes growing across the path or vines that love to entangle your feet? Trellising provides greater safety for the gardener around the plants. The practice can also increase growing space as the pathways can be narrower to a degree so long as maximum exposure to sunlight is ensured.

One of the primary goals of trellising raspberries is to train canes to be upright and largely uniform in orientation, providing better air circulation and exposure to sunlight. Vines are lifted off the ground and trained to a trellis for the same reasons. Not only that, but trellising can also boost production as the plants do not need to expend as much energy in developing sturdier canes and stalks with which to support the foliage and fruit.[6] Fruit production can be increased by significant amounts as a result. Plants and their fruit are healthy because they are away from pathogens and insect pests that overwinter in the soil.[7]

Fruit is heavy, as is the combined weight of foliage. The best trellises are sturdy, almost overbuilt. Posts should be either metal or wood and tall enough to meet the needs dictated by the plants and the training methods to be used. Crosswires can be twine, especially if they will be taken down at the end of the season to facilitate either pruning of canes or removal of vines from the trellis for overwintering. Wire is stronger and lasts for years and can support a heavier weight. Red raspberries can be readily supported by either material as the trellis is not supporting their entire weight. Should grape or kiwi vines not need to be laid down, then that is the route to go for these species. Hops that climb and twine can be supported by thick twine as the rough texture provides ideal grip for the vines. This is likewise true for any melons and other fruit of the squash family as their vines are easily damaged by wires. It is always wise to use earth anchors to tie down the crosswires for additional strength.

Red raspberries are best planted within a bed that is one to two feet (thirty to sixty centimetres) across. At the end of the bed, sink a post at each corner, at least one to two feet deep (thirty to sixty centimetres) into the soil. If the bed is longer than fifteen to twenty feet (four and a half to six metres), then additional posts should be used midway for structural integrity of the trellis. At the top of the posts, add a crosspiece to link the two posts together. Run the twine or wire between each post on both sides of the bed, starting at three feet (one metre) above soil level and every two feet (sixty centimetres) higher. The canes will grow within the trellis, but should they exhibit any attempt to evade their space, then pull them back and tie them to the supports.[8]

Grapes should be trellised in the same fashion, but only one post is required and should be centred in the middle of the bed rather than the two posts needed for red raspberries. Positioning of the crosswires is dependent on which training system is chosen. The high-wire cordon system is designed to grow a vine with a taller central stem, and with the arms of the plants supported by the top wire. Once the posts are in, string the upper layer of wire along the top, usually between 4 and 6 feet (1.2 to 1.8 metres) high. Lower wires are strung to support the plants as they grow to reach the top wire. Once at the top, the cordons are trained in either direction along the wires. Should the vertical shoot positioned system be chosen, then the first wire is positioned approximately three feet (one metre) above soil level, and once the stem reaches that level, the arms are trained along it in either direction. Succeeding "catch wires" are added as shoots are allowed to grow upwards from the main arms to the height that is desired.[9]

Kiwis have modified trellises along the lines of the vertical shoot positioned system used for grapes and may include a pergola if the climate permits the vines to overwinter high above ground.[10]

Hops are happy to clamber along any design of trellising, but do not underestimate their growing power. They are an herbaceous species and are cut back to the ground each year, but those vines can easily be twenty feet (six metres) long in a few months. Always plan for more growth than expected when designing a trellis for them.

Squash prefers a trellis that is composed of a frame, with two posts and a crosspiece, the width and height both dictated by the species and the gardener's desire.

The crosswires should be much closer together, approximately four inches (ten centimetres) apart, and be both vertical and horizontal to create squares, which provide numerous points to anchor the vines as well as integral support for the vines and developing fruit. Except for the smallest species such as cucumbers, squash fruit should also have auxiliary supports such as slings and hammocks so their fruit doesn't rip from the vine as it matures.

Tailor your trellis for each type of fruit you are growing and your growing conditions; also consider your specific weather conditions as to the positioning of the trellis to take into account prevailing winds and storms and the stress that they will put on both the trellis and its plants.

The results you will see in terms of fruit quality and production are more than worth the effort that goes into installing trellises and training the plants to them!—JM

It is essential to provide a support for grapevines to grow upon.

How can I control the suckers on fruit plants such as raspberries, sea buckthorn, and goji berries?

The propensity of some plants to spread via suckering can be, quite honestly, breathtaking in scope. Plant suckers are new roots and stems vegetatively formed from the meristem of roots on the parent plants. Even though some plants are a tad expressive when it comes to suckering, we may still want them in our gardens if the extra appendages are controlled in some way. The best way to treat unwanted suckers is to cut them down at ground level, wherever and whenever they occur. Don't use herbicides, as you may harm the parent plant through translocation of the chemical. To make your job lighter and easier, tackle suckers while they are new and tender.[11] — SN

Apple trees are also prone to suckering when under stress.

How should I prepare my fruit plants for winter?

I am not particularly keen on wrapping plants with burlap to protect them for winter—I would encourage everyone to instead try to seek out cold-hardy varieties for your region. Choose plants that are rated even hardier than your region's hardiness zone for better chances at success. Site your trees and shrubs properly out of drying winds, and if you can plan to avoid frost cracking, do so. That means keeping your plants as healthy and happy as possible throughout the year, watering them sufficiently during the growing season, and not stressing them out with poorly undertaken pruning.

At the same time, I come from a region (Calgary) where freeze-and-thaw cycles are legendary, and we sometimes don't have snow coverage for the entire winter. Drought and heat stress in the summer can be a huge issue in some years, which makes effective winter preparation even more crucial. Trees and shrubs in other parts of the prairies suffer the same fate. We need to give our fruit trees and shrubs every advantage we can going into winter, and that means properly preparing them for dormancy.

Wire mesh tree guards can help prevent critters such as voles from gnawing your fruit trees during the lean days of winter.

Here is your winter-prep checklist for your fruit trees and shrubs:

- [ ] Stop fertilizing your trees and shrubs by mid-summer. They don't need any nutrients going into the end of the season.

- [ ] Water your fruit trees and shrubs deeply as autumn creeps in. Pause on watering them from mid-September until mid- to late October, then give them a seriously good glug and put the hose away for the season.

- [ ] Clean up fruit and leaf litter from the base of the plants. This can help minimize the spread of diseases that may be found in the debris.

- [ ] Mulch the base of the trees with clean straw or wood chips. (See page 28–29 on how to effectively do this.)

- [ ] If you live in an area where wildlife such as deer, porcupines, and voles like to chow down on your trees during the winter, set up wire mesh tree guards to help prevent the damage. You can buy the guards at most garden centres or hardware stores.[12] —SN

Do I need to remove my grapevines from their trellises and lay them down on the ground before winter comes?

Prior to the release of cold-hardy or cold-climate grape varieties, bred to withstand temperatures below −35°F (−37°C), it was a maxim that all grapevines needed to be detached from their supports and laid on a bed of straw for insulation and then mulched heavily to protect the vines from above-ground frigid temperatures.

The greatest danger is to canes and spurs as grapes develop fruit on one-year wood, but also to the cordons (larger lateral branches) as well as the thicker trunks. It is not only the depth that temperatures plunge to; it is also the duration of extreme cold that is the concern. On the prairies, the huge variability of temperature swings within days of each other, not to mention hourly when a chinook is blowing, adds another layer of anxiety for the grower. In areas where snow cover remains consistent winter long, it provides a lot of insulation for the vines, but not so where literally feet of snow can disappear in a day or two.

To have the chance for years of successful harvests, do select a cultivar that is rated for zone 3 or 2 on the Canadian plant hardiness map. 'Valiant', which was developed in South Dakota in 1982, is considered the hardiest, followed by 'Beta', which dates to the 1880s. The Minnesota breeding program has several cultivars that have been showing up in our garden centres in the past few years. While they haven't stood the test of our winters for as long, 'Frontenac', 'Marquette', 'Frontenac Gris', and 'Swenson Red' are there for the trying.

Do select the best possible site, with tons of sun during the growing season, lots of air circulation, and well-draining soils, and no danger of frost pockets in spring or fall. A site where they are protected from chilling north winds come spring is a plus.

Some gardeners still do remove the vines and lay them down, especially in the most northerly regions. Others keep the vines attached to their supports but place cages (usually chicken wire) around the trunks and fill the cages with peat moss or leaves. If the first cordons are low enough to the ground, heaping leaves or straw over that lowest rung is providential. Still others leave their vines as they are and suffer minimal damage over many years.

Given the right cultivar and best site, it truly appears to come down to the area where you live and the winter conditions that normally prevail as to whether it is necessary to undertake the annual labour involved to lay the vines down.[13] —JM

Select the hardiest cultivars of grapes you can find for your region for best success.

Can I overwinter any of my fruit plants indoors in containers?

Cold-hardy fruit should overwinter in the ground for best success. The large volume of soil will protect the dormant roots through the season. Furthermore, for most fruit plants that are able to withstand our cold climate, a chilling period during dormancy is necessary. Haskap, for example, has a chilling period of between 750 and 1,000 hours, which means it needs to be exposed to temperatures of 45°F (7°C) or colder for that long each winter. If you are bringing your containers indoors, you won't likely be fulfilling that requirement.

If you are growing your perennial fruit plants in containers on your deck, for example, you can sink the container into the ground in late autumn and overwinter it in the insulating soil, then dig it back up again in the spring.[14] —SN

*Haskaps will not overwinter in containers indoors due
to their requirement for a long chilling period.*

Pruning

3

What is the best time to prune fruit trees and shrubs and why?

Ah, that depends on the goal and purpose of the pruning. Pruning is done to shape and train a tree. It is also performed to manage the energy of the tree and promote better fruit production.

If pruning to establish a newly planted tree or shrub, then it is performed just after planting, whenever that happens. Continue the training for the first few years and on a regular schedule. If pruning to encourage vigorous new growth, then late winter just before the trees have started to break dormancy is best. If the goal is to slow down or reduce the size of a tree that is growing too fast, then early summer after flowering is better. The worst time to prune is late summer and fall when the trees are maturing fruit and then need to go into dormancy without hindrance. Damaged, broken, and dangerous limbs should be pruned as soon as is feasible regardless of the season.

The reasons behind these considerations lie in the annual cycle of growth of woody plants. In the fall, they draw energy from their upper structures to be stored in their roots. Leaves fall, and water in tissues is withdrawn, increasing the sugar concentrations in cells as a mechanism to prevent cellular damage. The tree enters dormancy where little growth occurs, save in the roots, until the ground is fully frozen. By late winter, the soil is thawing and root growth resumes. Once trees start to come out of their dormancy, sap starts to rise into the upper structures. Then leaf and flower buds start to break, and we are into spring when the tree has lots of energy to devote to growth. By early summer, when trees are fully leafed out, the flowering is done, and the tree is developing fruit, the energy is slowing down. The cycle is complete.

Pruning in winter to just before trees come out of dormancy is often advocated as it is easy to see the structure and do proper pruning cuts. The drawback is that the wounds will not start to heal given the lack of growth occurring. The other consideration is that if pruning is quickly followed by a cold snap there can be winterkill damage to the limbs, which will definitely affect their healing and/or recovery. Best to wait until the really cold months of January and February are behind us.

Regular, judicious pruning is an important part of the maintenance and care of your fruit plants.

Timing your pruning to late winter or very early spring spurs vigorous growth. You have removed branches that are no longer pulling their weight. The tree then no longer needs to expend energy on those limbs and will direct it to the limbs you are promoting along with growing new shoots. Wounds heal fast in spring, with less chance of pathogens entering as the pollinators that may carry viruses are not yet out and about. Fungal fruiting bodies have not yet formed and bacteria are still dormant.

After spring leaf out and flowering, the tree energy is depleted. Pruning at this time will not result in huge growth and is often a boon when reducing the size of a too-tall tree is the aim or to dwarf the tree for ease of harvesting. Pruning not only dwarfs the upper structures, however; it will also affect the root system as not as much root mass is required to support the tree.

Mid-summer can be an excellent time to prune out new growth that is crossing, rubbing against other branches, or otherwise not in line with the desired scaffold. It is imperative to prune in summer if a diseased limb is discovered. Pruning in mid-summer can follow pruning in winter or very early spring to continue to bring an out-of-control tree back in line.

There are a couple of caveats to consider when making the decision to prune when a tree is flowering and maturing fruit. Pathogens that cause diseases such as fire blight can be transferred to new wounds through wind, water, and pollinators. Trees that are heavily pruned may prematurely drop fruit as they devote more energy to healing the cuts. If pruned too much, premature leaf drop may occur, which will impact the ability of the tree to replenish its energy store in time for fall and the end of that year's cycle.

Beyond the timing of pruning to accomplish the specific goals, do remember that any pruning should be done for good reason. Once gone, that limb will not grow back.[1] —JM

Why is it advised to train sour cherry plants as a shrub instead of in a tree form?

Sour cherry breeders on the prairies recommend keeping dwarf sour cherries pruned to a multi-stemmed shrub form in our climate over a tree or single-stemmed form to help protect the plants against dieback and winterkill. There are indications that the plants are more cold-hardy when allowed to grow as shrubs. And there are other benefits: dwarf sour cherries trained as shrubs may bear fruit one to two years earlier than those pruned as trees, plus they are much easier to harvest![2]—**SN**

While this is clearly a sour cherry tree (the single trunk gives it away!) there are some advantages to training dwarf sour cherry plants into shrub form.

What are fruit spurs?

Fruit spurs are stubby, almost thorn-like, slow-growing twigs that grow along older, lateral branches of some fruit trees. Usually less than six inches (fifteen centimetres) long, they have a wrinkled appearance because the internodes between each node are tiny, and the terminal bud scars are stacked on top of each other. Each spur contains both leaf and fruit buds, with the fruit bud being the terminal bud. Interestingly, spur-bearing varieties of fruit trees develop from mutations of standard tip-bearing varieties and are highly desired.

Very few fruit trees will bear fruit on new wood; those that do, such as figs and persimmons, mostly grow in warmer climes than the prairies. Some will bear fruit on second-year wood, on spurs that are very short, including peaches, plums, nectarines, and—that we should be so lucky—quinces.

Those that bear fruit on spurs that live for years are our apples, pears, and plums. In all instances, spurs develop from auxiliary buds.

There are varieties and cultivars of fruit trees that do not develop spurs and are called "tip-bearing," with the fruit developing at terminal buds at the end of each twig. It is generally agreed that spur-bearing varieties and cultivars are more productive, with the ability to bear fruit along lateral branches, making it easier to train and prune these types. Often trees that are smaller than the standard-sized species will be spur-bearing as most of the annual growth of the tree is directed to spur growth and not shoot growth. Before you invest in a tree, do decide if you want tip- or spur-bearing and determine if the cultivar you are interested in is a match.

Knowing if your tree is tip- or spur-bearing will dramatically affect how it is pruned. Tip-bearing trees should be trained to have a central leader with lateral branches developing up along the trunk. Alternatively, the tree could be trained to have a tulip shape without a central leader. Spur-bearing trees should be pruned to promote lateral branch development, creating a more open scaffold, with particular attention paid to the spurs so that they are evenly spaced along the branches. Not only will there be more air circulation, but also sunlight will be able to reach each fruit-bearing branch, and as a bonus the fruit is easier to harvest without balancing on ladders.

Knowing what spurs look like is vital, as it is easy to damage and even rip them off when harvesting and decrease fruit production for years to come.[3] —JM

The way your tree is pruned is dependent on whether or not it bears spurs.

When is a heading cut used during pruning?

Heading cuts are used to encourage denser, bushier growth on trees and shrubs. These cuts are made just above a bud or actively growing shoot to trigger new growth. These types of cuts are often done on shrubs if you want them to fill out and grow thicker. For safety considerations, they are not usually done with large branches on trees—a bunch of new growth can cause the tree to weaken and potentially become a problem during stormy weather.

To make a heading cut, select the area where you want to promote new growth. Think about the direction the new growth will go in before you cut. The new growth will appear in the same direction as the bud is currently growing. If the bud is pointed in a direction you don't want new growth to go, don't make that cut.

Once you've selected an ideal spot, use a pair of sharp pruners to cut about a quarter of an inch (six millimetres) above the bud. Traditionally, it was recommended that the cut should be made on a shallow slant in the direction away from the bud, as this would help prevent water from seeping into the cut surface and possibly facilitating the entrance of a pathogen. A slant is supposed to promote the movement of water away from the cut surface. The tricky part with taking that advice is that it might be tempting to make that slant too steep, which increases the surface area of the cut and opens the wound to potential disease problems. I would aim for a happy medium and make a nearly straight cut instead, with just a very slight slant. The goal should be to reduce the surface area of the cut, which means that the tree doesn't need to work so hard to compartmentalize a large wound. Once you've done a few of these cuts, you'll know the best place to make them.[4]—SN

When do you use thinning cuts during pruning?

Thinning cuts are the most common pruning cuts you will usually make. They are used to shape a tree or shrub or to remove dead or diseased branches or those that cross over each other. They are also used to open up the canopy of a tree or shrub to promote more air circulation or to allow sunlight through.

Here are thinning cuts in a nutshell:

Identify the branch you want to remove. Check where the branch collar is. (This is the rim where the branch connects to the trunk of the tree.) You never want to cut into the trunk as this might potentially wound the tree. Knowing where the branch collar is ensures you don't get too close.

For safety reasons, you will make your cuts in a very specific order. You don't want the branch to break and fall on you or someone else below! As well, if the branch is torn off the tree under its own weight, it will rip the bark wide open. This can result in a huge injury that can open the door to a slew of disease issues. First, use a pair of sharp pruners, bypass loppers, or a saw to make a partial cut on the bottom of the branch. Do not cut all the way through the branch—a halfway snip is all you want at this point. This cut should be made approximately twelve inches (thirty centimetres) outside the branch collar. Of course, if your branch isn't that lengthy, adjust this measurement to something smaller. The key is to have a bit of space to make safe cuts.

About two inches (five centimetres) outside that first tiny cut, you can cut the branch all the way through. Approach the cut from the top of the branch this time, not the bottom. The branch will fall.

You are now left with a long stick still affixed to the tree, and you don't want that. Make the final cut just outside the branch collar. This cut must be made from the top of the branch. Be extremely careful with this cut so you don't nick the trunk, but also bear in mind that you don't want to leave a short stub. If you cut too closely to the branch collar, sometimes the tree will respond by producing new shoots in the area. Remove them carefully and be sure not to cut into the branch collar again.[5]—SN

How are fruit trees espaliered?

Espalier is a method of training and pruning a tree or shrub so that it grows against a support such as a wall in a very specific and decorative way—in the shape of a fan, perhaps, or a candelabra, or even a diamond. It is highly artistic and incredibly space-saving, and it can take years to accomplish, so patience is required! On the prairies, apples and pears are commonly espaliered. Dwarf specimens are usually selected because they are easier to work with than a full-sized tree. Select a spot in full sun so your tree will perform at its healthiest and produce a decent yield of fruit. You will need to rig up a trellis or other support such as posts and wires against the wall to help train the tree. A three-tier horizontal cordon is an easy espalier form to attempt at first. You can set it up by using posts and three parallel horizontal wires. The uppermost wire will be positioned at the height of the mature tree, perhaps 4 feet (1.2 metres). The wires should be about 7 feet (2.1 metres) long to give the tree limbs room to stretch.

The tree you plant should be just a little guy, commonly called a whip—about twenty-four inches (sixty centimetres) tall. This is one time when you won't obey any typical recommendations of planting—you're going to deliberately put this seedling into the ground in summer so that the branches don't shoot up quickly. You want them to grow slowly. In the first fall, hack the whip back to about twenty inches (fifty centimetres) from the ground. Ensure you have at least three buds still on the tree below the cut. That sounds brutal, but it's part of the process. The following year, those buds you left will produce shoots, which you are going to loosely affix to the first wire. Let the little tree grow for the summer, then prune it again in autumn before the snow flies. Once again, ensure you have some buds below the cut, then top the central leader of the tree by taking it down to about thirty inches (seventy-five centimetres) above the ground. Tie the limbs of the tree to the lowest horizontal wire. And those are the first steps—you just keep repeating them every year until your tree has reached its mature height. Ensure your espaliered tree receives sufficient, regular watering throughout the growing season as all this pruning can be a tad stressful.

Once you have figured out this simple cordon, you can research some of the more elaborate forms and try your hand at them if you want to truly create something special. Living artwork for your garden—*and* you get fruit! It's a win-win![6]—SN

This espaliered apple tree is unique, beautiful, and full of delicious fruit!

How should I go about pruning my raspberry shrubs?

Before setting out to prune your raspberries, you need to know which sort you have in your garden. Summer-bearing (floricane) and fall-bearing, also known as everbearing (primocane), varieties are quite different in their life cycles, resulting in a different cycle of pruning.

The summer-bearing raspberries that we are most familiar with have a two-year cycle, with the "primocane" growing the first year, bearing leaves, and overwintering. The second year, the cane is now the "floricane" and soon flowers and sets fruit for harvesting come mid-summer. The canes will then die once the fruit is mature.

Everbearing raspberries are those that flower and set fruit on the primocane, with fruit maturing later in the season, typically late summer and into fall. In some climates, these everbearing raspberries can have two flushes of flowering and fruiting. The canes will overwinter and, in the second year, bear fruit again before dying off come that winter. Hence the name everbearing.[7]

Do prune summer-bearing raspberries once they have finished bearing their fruit. Remove the canes right back to the crown. This will give space for that year's primocanes to have all the air, sunlight, and nutrients they need in preparation for next year's crop. If any of this year's primocanes are weak or stunted, prune those out as well. Come the spring, after the danger from that last late killing frost is past, do tip prune the canes down to live wood if there is winter dieback. You also should—and this hurts—prune out canes so that they are evenly spaced for ease of harvesting and to prevent overcrowding and competition for resources.

Fall-bearing canes are dealt with much differently. After the flush of flowering and maturing fruit is finished for the season, prune the canes back by two-thirds. The following spring, these canes will bear fruit on the bottom two-thirds before dying. Prune the canes out at that point. Alternatively, sacrifice the second year's fruit by pruning all the canes down to their crowns in the fall each year.[8] Pruning simplified for sure!

Tip: use alternately coloured bits of wool, twist-ties, or surveyor's tape to identify the new primocanes each year for both summer- and everbearing raspberries to keep things straight. Yellow for year one and red for year two—and even green for the third year. It's a lifesaver for me as it eliminates any guesswork.

PS: Another pruning technique for summer-bearing raspberries is gaining ground. Cut every plant down to the crown every second year. It has the benefit of eliminating the work of reaching between canes to remove the floricanes. It also gives the plants a year off from flowering and maturing fruit, which not only boosts production the following year but works to build stronger and healthier plants overall as they do not have to expend the considerable energy it takes to mature fruit each year. It also helps control the insects and pathogens that might be present.[9] Plus you don't end up hot, bothered, and scratched!—JM

For better fruit production, prune raspberries according to their type.

Propagation

4

I've heard that apple trees grown from seeds will not be true to the parent plants. Is this true?

The apple (*Malus* spp.) is an ancient fruit. Its wild ancestor (*Malus sieversii*) is still to be found in central Asia, but the apple has travelled the world for upwards of 4,000 years. Through natural mutations, called sports, along with selective breeding, you can hardly recognize the apple (*Malus domestica*) we eat today from its ancestors. New varieties seem to come on the market every year but are mostly the product of hybridization.

These hybrids are vegetatively reproduced, which is to say cloned through grafting. It is the only way to ensure consistency of a variety.

The thing about apples is that they require cross-pollination to be fertilized. The agents in question are bees, who visit multitudes of apple trees in their quest for pollen. A blossom that goes on to produce a mature fruit will contain seeds with the DNA from both parents, and it can be radically different from its parents. In other words, apples do not breed *true to type*, even though they are open-pollinated. In fact, there is a better than even chance in urban gardens that the other parent is a crabapple (*M. baccata* or *M. sylvestris*).

So, if you would like to grow a specific variety, the best advice is to purchase a sapling of that variety. But if you are up for an experiment, by all means, collect seed from the apple you are munching.

Rather than just scattering seeds around willy-nilly like the fictionalized legend of Johnny Appleseed (he was actually a rather eccentric nurseryman), you should collect seeds with all the bits of apple cleaned off and examine them to make sure that the seed coat is intact. Apple seeds have a germination rate of only around 30 percent, so collect quite a few. Then place them in a container that has some air holes with either damp sand or dampened moss. Put them in the fridge for six to twelve weeks. Once they are out of the refrigerator, pot them up in a soilless mix and place them in a warm, sunlit location. When you have a few good-sized seedlings, they can be transplanted outside (after hardening off). This is a long-term project as it can take a decade for your new trees to produce fruit that will either be a dud or a brand-new delicious apple variety.[1] —JM

How can I propagate my berry plants using layering?

Some fruit species naturally propagate themselves through layering. Strawberries with their "stolons" (horizontal stems running above ground) are an example. Wherever a node (growing point) touches the soil adventitious roots will form, root into the soil, and create daughter plants—a simple and effective form of layering that involves no work for gardeners, except for snipping the runner at some point and planting the daughter where you would like her to be.

A few woody species, primarily in the *Ribes* genus, can be propagated using layering as they, too, naturally will root wherever a stem ends up touching the ground long enough for roots to form. Gooseberries (with thorns) and currants (without them thankfully) both have this ability, and we can take advantage of it by deliberately bending stems down to the ground and anchoring them to promote rooting.

Currants are readily propagated by layering.

Tip layering involves selecting a likely looking stem, then bending it down so that the tip reaches a small hole that you have dug—perhaps three or four inches (eight to ten centimetres) deep—and inserting the tip right into it. Cover the hole up and make sure that the tip won't come loose. I sometimes use a rock or two to buttress the stem in place for the first few weeks. But make sure to remove them smartish. The tip will continue growing down into the soil for a bit but then, because it knows which way is up, will take a sharp upward bend and exit the hole in short order. Roots will grow at the bottom of the bend, and once the stem is snipped off where it first entered you now have a new plant. In our cold soil, it is a good idea to leave the stem attached to the main plant over the winter and snip it come spring.

Simple layering is the same as tip layering except that the stem is simply bent down and anchored onto the surface of the soil. To aid root growth, nick the stem at the point it touches the soil—once again, I use the odd rock or two to keep the stem in contact for the first while.

Other berries can also be propagated in this fashion. The *Rubus* genus, which includes raspberries that have upright canes, along with brambles such as blackberry, loganberry, and thimbleberry that naturally create thickets through underground runners, can all have their canes bent over to propagate through layering.[2]—JM

Why are fruit trees commonly grafted? Is there an easy way to graft them?

Fruit trees are commonly grafted to get the most desirable plant for the climate they are growing in. A grafted tree is composed of two parts: the rootstock, or base of the tree that is made up of roots and trunk, and a scion, the upper portion, which has branches and will bear flowers and fruit. The rootstock is selected for characteristics such as cold hardiness, disease resistance, and size, while the scion is chosen for traits such as beautiful flowers and flavourful fruit. Sometimes grafting is done to obtain a small-sized tree for a tiny yard; other times, more than one type of apple or other fruit might be grafted onto a tree to get multiple delicious varieties that ripen at different times. The rootstock and the scion must be compatible plants, within the same family. The procedure is usually done in late winter through early spring when the plants' sap is running.

There are numerous ways to graft a plant, but a common and simple method is the cleft graft. Your rootstock and scion should be similar in size in order to match up the cambium (outer) layers of the pieces. Give it a try:

1.   Trim the rootstock. Use the sharpest pair of pruners you can get; these cuts need to be clean and perfect.

2.   Find the bottom end of the scion. You need this part to line up with the part you just trimmed on the rootstock. Don't flip the scion upside down or you aren't likely to have success with this particular graft. Trim about 1 inch (2.5 centimetres) off the bottom end of the scion so you have a fresh cut to work with. Ensure you have a minimum of three fresh buds on the scion, then trim the top portion, too. You just need a nice fresh cut on the end.

3.   At the bottom of the scion, cut a wedge on two sides. The wedge needs to be approximately the same height on each side — don't make one side bigger than the other. This is the part that you are going to insert into the rootstock, so be tidy about your whittling.

4. Slice the rootstock down the centre of the branch you are graft-ing to. Your cut should be the length of the wedge you just made on the scion.

5. Carefully insert the scion wedge into the cut in the rootstock. It should be a snug fit. Line up those cambium layers!

6. Seal your graft to keep it in place and hopefully prevent infec-tion. Grafting tape can be purchased at a garden centre and used for this job.

If your graft is successful, you'll welcome new growth on the scion in several weeks. You probably won't get flowers and fruit on the scion for a few years, but the wait is worth it![3]—sn

It's easy to spot the bulge where the scion and the rootstock meet on this grafted apple tree.

Check out all the graft unions on this multi-grafted tree!

How do I propagate fruit plants using softwood cuttings?

Softwood cuttings are the easiest of all the woody stem cuttings to root successfully because you are using the new stem growth early in the year when it is still soft and succulent and has not yet started to lignify or become woody.

Propagation through softwood cuttings should be done between May and July. Choose shoots or twigs that are still flexible and have a graduation of leaf size from largest at the base to smallest at the tip.

You want to start by watering the plant a few days before so that it is well hydrated. Early in the morning, when the stems are at maximum turgidity from the cool temperatures overnight, select stems that are growing from a leader and cut approximately 1 inch (2.5 centimetres) below a leaf node. The cutting doesn't need to be too long, say four to six inches (ten to fifteen centimetres), because the more leaves on the cutting, the more it will be prone to wilting.

Remove the leaves from the node, then slice a thin strip of bark from the bottom inch below the node. This action will trigger the cutting to grow root cells. It is recommended that you coat the bottom with a root compound that contains the plant hormone auxin, which further stimulates root growth. Gently insert cuttings about an inch to an inch and a half deep (five to eight centimetres) into a container—such as a clay pot or milk jug with drainage holes—filled with growing medium. Never use garden soil, but rather a mix of one part peat to one part perlite or one part sand to one part vermiculite. Rather than watering from the top, set the pot into a tray filled with water and allow the water to wick up into the growing medium.

The next step is key as you will want the cutting to have humid air around it so that it doesn't transpire too much while it is rooting. Cover the cuttings with a plastic dome, large enough that it doesn't touch the leaves. Using a four- or even two-litre plastic milk jug as a cloche is a cost-effective option. Cut the bottom off and add extra air holes at the top and you are in business. I often tape the top to the container to have a nice, neat unit. There are inexpensive premade ones, too. Place the container in indirect light and monitor the conditions to ensure excess humidity does not build up. The growing medium should be kept moist, but not soaking wet. After six weeks or so, gently tug on the cuttings. If they resist being pulled out, they are rooted!

Pot them individually into larger pots with soilless growing medium to grow for the rest of the season. Just before winter comes, sink the pot into a handy garden bed to overwinter. Plant them out next year when they are at the size you want. You could also opt to grow them on for a further year in their pots.

Most shrubs can be propagated by this method, and a few trees, and it is most appropriate for hybrid varieties that would not be true to type if grown from seed.[4]—JM

Sea buckthorn is readily propagated by softwood cuttings.

Pests, Diseases, and Physiological and Environmental Issues

5

In our book *The Prairie Gardener's Go-To for Pests and Diseases*, we extensively covered several of the baddies that affect our plants, from slugs to deer to cytospora canker, fire blight, black knot, and everything in between. Here, in *The Prairie Gardener's Go-To for Fruit*, we've narrowed our focus to specific fruit-related issues beyond what we explored in *Pests and Diseases*.

It looks like a creepy-crawly is feeding on the buds of my saskatoon shrubs. What is this, and how can I stop it from ruining my chances at getting fruit?

Wherever saskatoons (*Amelanchier alnifolia*) are growing there is the chance that the saskatoon bud moth (*Epinotia bicordana*) will be present.

These are small grey-black and brown moths. As soon as they come out in early spring, they lay their eggs at the base of fruit buds and between stems. The eggs hatch two weeks later and immediately move to the developing flower buds to feed. Signs of their presence include tiny holes in the buds that may seep liquid. The buds will fall off to the touch. The larvae become yellow green and can be easily spotted by this point. As the larvae reach maturity, they weave webs between petals and surrounding leaves, and by early fall they crawl into the enclosure to pupate. But the damage is long done by then with little to no fruit for the season.

The best protection for your plants is to prevent the adults from laying eggs, usually in April. If possible, use a fine mesh to cover the shrubs. It can be removed by mid-May. BT kurstaki (*Bacillus thringiensis* subsp. *kurstaki*) is also an option, especially if you happen to have badly infested shrubs. It may not prevent damage for this year's crop but will prevent the larvae from pupating and becoming adults for next year. BT is a bacterium found in soils worldwide and does not produce toxins that are harmful to humans. The bacterium produces a protein crystal that, when consumed by the larvae, releases toxins that paralyze the larvae, and death ensues.

Saskatoon bud moth is the bane of commercial saskatoon growers, and in the home garden it may become a problem. Monitoring your shrubs for sight of adults in early spring and signs and symptoms thereafter will go a long way to preventing problems for the home gardener.[1] —JM

I think I have scale insects on my apple trees. Is there anything I can do?

Apple scale or San Jose scale (*Quadraspidiotus perniciosus*) is well named. It is a pernicious insect that arrived from Asia over a century and a half ago and promptly became a serious pest. It has spread all over the United States and into British Columbia and Ontario. While it isn't widespread on the prairies, it is only a matter of time as our climate moderates. It behooves us to learn to recognize its signs and symptoms before it becomes the problem that it is elsewhere, for it can infect not only apple but pear and all the stone fruit. Not only that, but it can affect berry shrubs and even ornamental trees and shrubs.

It is related to oystershell scale (*Lepidosaphes ulmi*), a pest that most prairie gardeners are all too familiar with—both belong to the scale insect family, Diaspididae. It is a tiny insect that by itself can't do much damage, but it produces thousands of offspring in a single season—two generations that rapidly set to work to suck the life out of the plant.

It is the adult females that attach themselves like limpets. Once established, she is wingless, eyeless, legless, and not mobile. She produces live young, called crawlers, that are 0.02 inches (0.5 millimetres) long. These tiny yellow crawlers have six legs, eyes, antennae, and a sucking beak. Once they migrate to another site on the plant, they attach themselves and start excreting a waxy coating that covers their body and hardens as a white scale that turns black and finally grey. The yellow-tan males can fly, but they are hard to see as they are tiny with large wings and antennae.

Favourite locations to initially settle are under the scales of bark on trunks where they cannot be readily discovered, but they will expand to cover any surface. Most often the first sign of a problem is on the fruit, which develops bright red spots with a slightly sunken indentation that enlarge and fade to pink over time. Further inspection will discover the scales on twigs, branches, and trunk, with dead areas on the bark or entire limbs girdled. Leaves may have small brown dead spots. Fruits on affected plants are small and immature and do not develop their proper colour. They may split open and have a musty smell. Leaves may not fall in autumn, and over time twigs—and then branches—will die. The plant will weaken, and if the infestation is unchecked it will die.

Control is difficult, so monitoring your plants is important for those first few crawlers or scales. Natural predators are few and are not likely to eliminate an infestation. Dormant oil is our best course of action, applied generously in spring as soon as crawlers are spotted and when they are vulnerable. Do prune out heavily infested branches and twigs. Heavily affected trees and shrubs may require the services of an arborist as there are chemical controls, but that action of last resort is not undertaken lightly.

In Calgary, every homeowner with a cotoneaster hedge knows the signs of an infestation of oystershell scale and knows that regularly cutting the plants back to the ground and allowing them to regrow is the best course of action. For apple trees that are severely infected, removal may be the last recourse to prevent this scale from becoming endemic. We are wise if we learn about this insect now and know the signs and symptoms of its arrival and the best and early course of action to ensure our apple and other fruit trees and shrubs are kept safe. Apple scale will not be the first nor the last new insect to the prairies as our climate becomes more hospitable to pests that were kept away by our previously severe and prolonged winters.[2] —JM

Something is eating the leaves of my pear trees. What could it be?

Many years ago, I once told an entomologist that I thought slugs were ugly. He responded, of course, that slugs aren't insects, and went on to say they are beautiful and necessary too.

Pear slugs aren't actually slugs; they just look like them, and we might be forgiven for thinking them ugly because they are the larvae of the pear sawfly, also known as black sawfly (*Caliroa cerasi*), an accidentally introduced species from Europe that has been with us for some centuries. They affect not only pear and cherry trees but species from apples to mountain ash, cotoneaster to saskatoons.

Sawflies are small, shiny, black wasps, only a quarter of an inch (five millimetres) long. You barely notice that they are present, and if you spot them you are forgiven for thinking they are another fly. The female adults emerge in early to mid-summer and lay their eggs in slits on the undersides of leaves that they cut with sawlike ovipositors. About two weeks later, the eggs hatch and the larvae emerge in one of five "instars" (developmental stages) before they drop to the soil to burrow deeply and pupate in cocoons safe below ground level for the winter. The first we see of the slimy, olive-green larvae is somewhat tadpole in shape with a larger head than tail. They migrate to the top of the leaves and start munching, literally rasping off the surfaces of the leaves. By the time they reach the final instar they look like small yellow-orange caterpillars with ten legs, and the leaves of heavily affected trees and shrubs may look bleached or scorched or have reddish patches from their feeding. Skeletonizing may also occur, which impacts the ability of the plant to photosynthesize. The damage is often minor, though severe infestations may weaken a tree or shrub if it continues over successive years, affecting the numbers of flowers and causing reduced fruit size and premature defoliation.

Often the first sign that pear sawfly has found a home in your garden is yellowish spots on leaves in mid-July. Looking closely, you may see the tiny, mucus-coated black larvae or later instars up to the caterpillars toward fall, when damage to the leaves is more apparent.

Your choice for action, if you chose to act at all, may simply be washing off the larvae with a strong blast of water and following up with lightly cultivating the soil around the plant to disturb any larvae that are already pupating. Problem solved.

Should numbers of larvae be high enough to require stronger action, insecticidal soap applied to the top and bottom of the foliage will likely do the trick. There are some pesticides available if the problem becomes severe. Please do consult with an arborist before taking that step as the chemicals are not specific to this sawfly and will kill other, beneficial insects as well.

Pear sawfly and all the other sawflies of the Tenthredinidae family are important as pollinators. There are several species native to North America and the prairies. They pollinate our vegetables, fruit, and ornamental species as well as many species in our forests, woodlands, meadows, and riparian habitats.

While we may not want their larvae skeletonizing our favourite fruit trees and other plants in the garden, they are an essential part of the biodiverse environment and should be valued for their roles as adults.[3]—JM

Pear sawfly larvae can do a number on your fruit trees, but the adult flies can act as pollinators. This is an example of why we don't always need to take action when we see a critter bugging our plants.

Disgusting! My cherry fruit is full of what appear to be worms. How can I prevent my fruit from being destroyed?

The cherry fruit fly (*Rhagoletis* spp.) is a relatively new pest in Canada. The larvae completely ruin cherry fruit by feeding on it from within—to add insult to injury, they also deposit their wastes inside the fruit. The pests are irritating for home gardeners, to be sure, and devastating for orchard growers.

There are a few different species of cherry fruit fly, but their general appearance is similar, as is their behaviour. The adults are small (about 0.15 inches or 4 millimetres long) black flies. Their wings are clear and feature several dark bands. The female cherry fruit fly emerges from her winter vacation home in the soil in May through July and lays her eggs in cherry fruit. The larvae hatch inside the cherry fruit and feed for up to six weeks, after which they crawl out of the fruit, drop to the ground, and pupate beneath the soil. The insects can easily overwinter in our climate—and, in some cases, stay there in "diapause" (suspended development) for up to three years.

Unfortunately, without resorting to chemical use, there isn't a lot a home gardener can do to diminish cherry fruit fly infestations. Pheromone sticky traps can be helpful, but it's best to consult a certified arborist for treatment.[4]—SN

One word for these guys: yuck!

Some of the fruit on plants in my garden are full of larvae: my strawberries, sour cherries, and plums are affected. What can I do to prevent my harvest from being ruined?

Spotted wing drosophila (*Drosophila suzukii*) is a relatively new insect pest on the prairies, first making appearances here about a decade ago (and in warmer British Columbia a little earlier than that). This tiny (0.07 to 0.11 inches or 2 to 3 millimetres long) fruit fly is native to Southeast Asia and, due to its disagreeability with cold climates, wasn't a problem until recently. Unfortunately for us, it has discovered that it enjoys our nice hot summers, as well as many of the berries and fruit we grow. It can be difficult to tell apart spotted wing drosophila from other fruit flies, as both the males and the females are brown and they have transparent wings like other fruit flies. The males, however, have a dark spot on the tip of each wing, and two black bands on their legs. The females, who need to slice into fruit peels to lay their eggs, have a toothed ovipositor that does the job.

Unlike many other species of fruit fly, which, happily (for gardeners everywhere), lay eggs in and feed primarily on fallen fruit, spotted wing drosophila goes after the good fruit, the lovely specimens on the plants that we are looking forward to harvesting. (They will also infest fallen fruit if they feel like doing so.) The adult females lay their eggs inside the fruit. This is a procedure that can take a very long time—anywhere from ten days to a whopping two months, during which they lay between seven and sixteen eggs per day. The larvae hatch in as little as two hours (or up to seventy-two), then they start munching. Between six and twenty-eight days from the time they are hatched, the larvae pupate, then emerge as adults. Because the females lay their eggs using a successive approach, you can see how this can all quickly get out of hand in a growing season. (In British Columbia, it appears that the flies can produce five generations per year if the temperatures are suitable. On the prairies, that may not happen, but we're likely to still get a few generations per growing season.) Adult flies that emerge in the autumn are capable of overwintering.

Spotted wing drosophila don't simply go after one type of host plant, either: strawberries, sour cherries, apricots, and plums are all fair game, as are many other cultivated fruit as well as those growing in the wild. No one is going to eat fruit that is full of larvae, and orchard growers cannot bring it to market. Not only that, but once the fruits are damaged, the wounds in them open the door for pathogens such as botrytis.

Control for spotted wing drosophila is tricky for home gardeners. Orchard growers who do not want to take a huge hit for losses — and who do not grow organically — will use commercial chemical sprays to try to deal with the economic hit. Otherwise, meticulous sanitation practices are necessary. Clean up fallen fruit litter and plant debris from the base of the plants. If you notice that the fruit is going soft due to the presence of larvae, destroy the ruined fruit by crushing it. Cool weather makes these beasties less active and less inclined to destroy your fruit, but of course we want nice warm weather for our plants to produce excellent yields. There isn't a lot of good news when it comes to successfully controlling spotted wing drosophila using organic methods — not yet anyway.[5] —SN

There are some strange growths on my chokecherry fruit. What is up with that?

If you are spotting some weirdly shaped berries in among the clusters of fruit from your chokecherries or saskatoons, you might be seeing galls created by insects. The galls look like grotesquely oversized berries that are more pear-shaped than round. The galls are green as they form but eventually turn red before they fall off the plant. The fruit that has been turned into galls will not contain any seeds.

The tiny critters that modify berries in this way are chokecherry gall midges (*Contarinia virginianae*). In the spring, adult females lay their eggs in the flowers of chokecherries or saskatoons. The berries begin to develop as usual in the summertime, and the miniature yellow-orange maggots time their hatch so they can begin feasting on the fruit. (The berries, incidentally, also make great little Airbnbs for the larvae while they dine! Several larvae may indulge in the luxurious accommodations afforded by each gall.) Around the end of July, the larvae will finally finish eating, and they'll abandon the now hollow berries in favour of pupating on the ground and getting ready to produce the next generation the following year.

There isn't a lot that can be done to prevent chokecherry gall midges from doing their dirty work, other than to practise excellent sanitation: clean up all the leaf and fruit litter off the ground, especially in autumn, as this might also eliminate some of the pupating insects. If you spot the galls on the trees, cut them off and destroy them. This will help pare down the population.[6]—SN

The leaves on my fruit plants are covered in spots. What causes this? Is it harmful?

Leaf spots are a dime a dozen in the horticultural world—there are so many different kinds, and they affect so many different plants, that it's quite likely, if you garden, you've already encountered at least one. There are two types, bacterial and fungal, with fungal leaf spots being the less harmful and the more prevalent. Most are host specific, meaning that each pathogen will attack only plants in the same family. Leaf spot diseases cause defoliation of plants with varying severity and duration. If only a few leaves are affected and the infection lasts only a year or two, you probably don't have to worry too much and don't have to do anything other than minimize the stress on your plants. If a significant portion of the total foliage is lost, and this occurs every year, then you will have to act. If the infected plants are large trees, a certified arborist can diagnose what type of leaf spot you have and recommend a treatment. In some cases, the plant may require removal. Over time, even the mildest of leaf spots can weaken the plants and make them vulnerable to attacks from other pathogens and pests.

Identifying leaf spots in a general way is fairly simple; the leaves exhibit spots, either regular or irregular in shape, large or small. The spots will be a different colour than the leaf: yellow, red, purple, black, brown, white, and so on. The spots may be ringed or not. They can be raised on the surface of the leaf, or they can be flush. For some fungal leaf spots, the spores may even be visible (until they are dispersed by rain or irrigation water). You may be able to narrow down your ID if you know what type of fruit plant you have and which types of spots affect that particular species. If you can't figure out which spot is which, don't fret—you can still do something!

Most leaf spots can overwinter in leaf litter, even in our cold climate, so rake up those fallen leaves before the snow flies. Do not compost them. Water your trees and shrubs sufficiently and at the base of the plants so that fungal spores and bacteria are not splashed upwards into the plant, and maintain good air circulation through the plant by pruning. Use mulch to suppress weeds, conserve soil moisture, and maintain consistent soil temperatures. If you know that your plant has a leaf spot, hold off on the high-nitrogen fertilizer so that you aren't promoting tender green leaf growth only to lose it. If you must replace your infected plants, look for leaf spot–resistant species or cultivars.[7]—SN

This spotting on the leaves of a hawthorn tree is caused by a fungus called Gymnosporangium globosum.

My apples are scabby. What is going on?

Apple scab (*Venturia inaequalis*) on our precious apples (*Malus* spp.) looks exactly like its name: corky, scabby lesions on fruit that can literally split open the developing fruit, making them inedible. Leaves develop small, velvety, olive-brown spots, first on the undersides but then on top, that progress to full-scale necrosis, stunting and twisting their growth and ability to photosynthesize and causing premature leaf drop. The disease also progressively weakens the trees and makes them prone to other pathogens and insect infestation, not to mention reducing their ability to withstand the onslaughts of winter.

A fungus, which by the way can infect crabapples too, it also has strains that infect mountain ash (*Sorbus* spp.), pears (*Pyrus* spp.) and cotoneaster (*Cotoneaster* spp.), all of which are members of the rose family (Rosaceae). Its life cycle is key to being able to control it and minimize periodic or ongoing infections.

The fungus overwinters in fallen, infected apple and crabapple leaves. Come spring thaw, the fungus develops "pseudothecia" on the decaying leaves, which in turn develop "ascospores" that await a rainstorm to trigger their release by wind up into the tree above or others nearby showing the first new leaves. Even a heavy dew or shower can be enough of a trigger when the ascospores are ready. The spores need a period of several hours on wet leaves to infect them, along with warm temperatures of around 70°F (20°C), and then between ten and twenty-eight days later the first signs of infection appear. The lesions on the leaves in turn develop fruiting bodies called "conidia," which cause infections later in the season that can directly infect developing fruit, causing premature drop or those ugly lesions. Wet and warm springs and summers provide the ideal conditions for multiple waves of infection.

They say an ounce of prevention is worth a pound of cure—except in the case of *this* fungus, there is no cure, so prevention is all. It is a matter of managing the disease triangle to the best advantage. We can do nothing to manage the weather, but we can manage the host by selecting scab-resistant varieties of both apple and crabapple cultivars if your area has had occurrences. Most provinces across Canada do, and it is a significant commercial pathogen for British Columbia and Ontario apple growers. On the prairies, it was rare before 2010, but now it is increasingly common.[8]

What we can manage is the environmental conditions through our cultural practices. Do thoroughly clean up and dispose of infected fruit and leaves in the garbage or alternatively bury or burn them, and preferably before the first snowfall come fall. If the tree has been infected early in the season, remove any fallen leaves or dropped fruit when it occurs. When planting either a crabapple or apple, do provide enough space for it to reach maturity without being crowded. Train the tree so that its branches are well spaced for maximum airflow. Should any water sprouts form on lateral branches, remove them promptly. Ditto for any suckers growing from the base of the trunk. Do ensure that the soil around the tree is well mulched. Even better, consider creating a polyculture of other species, both shrubs and herbaceous plants, as the biodiverse community will work to ensure the health of the tree.

The temptation is to treat a tree with an active infection with a fungicide. But this is not recommended unless the tree has been infected for three consecutive years and is showing signs of weakening. Nor should fungicide be applied if the fruit is meant for eating. In all cases do consult and use an arborist trained to choose the right fungicide and apply it without danger to you and the environment. This is definitely a last resort and will not serve to prevent reinfection the next time the apple scab spores are drifting in the wind.[9]—JM

There are blisters on the undersides of the leaves of my currants and gooseberries. What causes this, and should I be concerned?

White pine blister rust (*Cronartium ribicola*), or WPBR for short, is an invasive species of fungus introduced to North America in the early 1900s. Its hosts are five-needle pines, including white (*Pinus strobus*), limber (*P. flexilis*), whitebark (*P. albicaulis*), and western white (*P. monticola*), all of which are significant commercial forestry species. A pine infected with the rust exhibits orange swellings, followed by cankers that girdle the trunk. Blisters then form on top of the cankers that split open to release the orange spores in spring. Tree death occurs above the site of the cankers.

Interesting, you say, but what does this fungus have to do with currants and gooseberries?

Unfortunately, WPBR requires an alternative host to complete its life cycle, which happens to be species of the *Ribes* genus, including of course our currants and gooseberries. Once the infected pine releases "aeciospores" some three to six years after its initial infection, it is then the turn of the alternate host, whose leaves will be infected and subsequently display orange pustules on the undersides. The pustules will mature by early fall and release "basidiospores," which go on to infect a new generation of pines.[10]

The fungus doesn't seriously damage currants and gooseberries, but the devastation to white pines prompted many controls on the planting of *Ribes* species. In the northern United States there are still existing bans on planting European blackcurrant (*R. nigrum*) unless it is a known cultivar that is resistant to WPBR. In Canada and the United States, forestry practices to reduce populations of native and non-native species of *Ribes* are common.[11]

Considerable work has been done over the decades to develop WPBR-resistant cultivars of both white pine and *Ribes*, with considerable success.

As responsible gardeners, we are encouraged to plant only resistant species and cultivars. Luckily there are many!

Our native golden currant (*R. aureum*) has the highest resistance. The native clove currant (*R. odoratum*) has high resistance, especially 'Crandall' that dates back to 1888. The wax currant (*R. cereum*) is also usefully resistant, as is the Red Lake currant (*R. rubrum* 'Red Lake'), which is commonly found in most nurseries. The Primus white currant (*R. rubrum* 'Primus') is also highly resistant. Should you wish to plant European blackcurrant (*R. nigrum*), which is the least resistant and naturally the most desired currant for gardeners, do look for cultivars such as 'Consort', developed in 1948 by Agriculture Canada. 'Titania', bred in Sweden, has 'Consort' as its parent. Saskatchewan-bred 'Willoughby' was released in 1957 and has been discovered to be highly resistant. The Ben series of blackcurrants have been developed by the Scottish Crop Research Institute and have some resistance to WPBR, with 'Ben Nevis' the most resistant, followed by 'Ben Sarek'.

Gooseberries (*R. uva-crispa*) have many cultivars resistant to WPBR, and they are also the ones that have been bred to provide bigger berries and a less tart taste as a bonus. Do look for any of 'Hinnomaki Red' in particular, but also 'Pixwell' and 'Poorman'.

Jostaberries (*R. × nidigrolaria*) are a cross between a blackcurrant and a gooseberry. They don't have thorns and bear plenty of delicious fruit. They are also resistant to white pine blister rust.

There are few tools in the tool box to control this damaging fungus. Good cultural practices such as widely spacing plants and watering deeply with mulch to hold moisture in the soil are important to ensure the health of our currants and

gooseberries, which in turn provides them with excellent defences against WPBR. Most importantly though is our responsibility to plant WPBR-resistant species and cultivars. Together, these practices will cut out the alternate host for this disease and reduce its incidence in our white pines.[12]—JM

Golden currants are more resistant to white pine blister rust than many other types of currants.

I'm noticing wilting and dieback in my grape plants. What could be wrong?

Verticillium wilt affects many different types of plants, including fruit such as grapes. The pathogens *V. dahliae* and *V. albo-atrum* are responsible for causing this deadly fungal disease. They live in the soil and enter the plant through its feeder roots. The fungal spores, called microconidia, travel through the xylem of the plant and introduce new hyphae throughout, effecting a highly progressive spread of infection. The plant will have a difficult time taking up water and nutrients. The worried gardener then starts to notice symptoms such as the sudden curl, wilting, and yellowing of foliage. The leaves may eventually turn reddish, then drop prematurely. Next up: the inner parts of the stems and branches may discolour and darken, and the stems and branches of the plants will begin to die.

Affected plants will tend to exhibit symptoms in the spring or fall when the temperatures are cooler. The disease isn't as active in the heat of summer. Unfortunately, once it has taken hold of your plants, you can't do anything about it—and it can stay in the soil for many years, even if you have yanked the plants out. If it kills your plants, you shouldn't plant another species that is susceptible to verticillium wilt in their place unless you sterilize the soil through solarization.

If you recognize that your plants have verticillium wilt, be prepared to deal with the fact that they likely won't live long. You can keep them going a bit longer by ensuring they are regularly watered and have sufficient nutrients at the correct time of year (for fruit plants, that usually means once a year, in the spring). Prune the plants only when necessary (except to remove dead or diseased wood) and sterilize your pruners after each cut. Do not compost any of the trimmings.

If you are concerned about the potential for verticillium wilt to take down some of your fruit plants, consider purchasing varieties that are less susceptible.[13]—SN

The leaves on my raspberries are curling. What is wrong with them?

There are so many reasons why leaves curl on plants, and sometimes it is a process of elimination to get to the root of the problem.

Abiotic or environmental reasons include excessive heat and/or drought, which can be enough of a reason for leaves to curl under. Do check soil moisture to determine if it has enough moisture at least one foot (thirty centimetres) down. In the summer of 2021, the extreme heat that prevailed in the Calgary area meant it was difficult to combat loss of moisture from plants and soil, and we seemed to do nothing but water. Mulch will help to conserve soil moisture if that is the issue.

Herbicide drift can be another unwelcome reason. Many species, including tomatoes and raspberries, are very sensitive to herbicide drift. It might be wise to check to see if there are any municipal signs around indicating that they have sprayed for weeds. Neighbours may also have sprayed herbicide and it came over the fence. There is nothing to do if that is the case but wait for the plants to grow past the damage—and, if fruit was forming, to discard it.

There are unfortunately several insects that find raspberry leaves succulent, with curly leaves often the result. Aphids, leafrollers, leafhoppers, and psyllids all are drawn to the strong, succulent, and aromatic leaves. Check the undersides of leaves to scout for any signs of insects present, perhaps wrapped up inside the leaves, webbing, or signs of their frass (the excretion of insect larvae).

If all these abiotic and biotic causes of the curling can be eliminated, it is time to consider one of the viruses that raspberries host. It is spread via an insect vector, the American large raspberry aphid (*Amphorophora agathonica*) or the European version (*A. idaei*), but also via plant debris that is not cleaned up, suckers, and roots, plus soil, even on the bottoms of shoes and on our tools.

Raspberry mosaic virus complex, also known as raspberry leaf curl, is not one but two viruses, each with multiple strains.[14] While no raspberry varieties are immune to the various strains, red raspberries may only show faint chlorotic mottling of leaves, especially on older leaves. However, symptoms can include downward-curling or puckered leaves that show evidence of chlorosis and/or blistering, especially if the early part of the season has been on the cool side. Flowers are likely to be malformed and the fruit dry and crumbly. Canes are stunted, and there is overall a decline in vigour. While the first year may see mild symptoms, generally the virus will destroy the plants within three years.

The bad news? There is no cure. Do eliminate all other causes and/or confirm your diagnosis with a plant tissue test, ideally in spring when they are actively growing.

Remove all the infected plants, likely the entire stand or row, but if you discovered it before it spread, then possibly only a couple of plants have been infected. Destroy them through burning or double bag them and put them in the garbage.

When replanting, ensure that you are using certified disease-free stock, with preferably red varieties over purple or black ones, which are significantly more susceptible. Avoid planting in the same location, with an ideal distance of fifty feet (fifteen metres) from the original site, as the virus can remain viable in the soil for years. Monitor for aphids, using yellow sticky cards, and take steps to eliminate any that appear through manual controls. Practise careful hygiene with tools and footwear and mulch the plants.[15] —JM

This raspberry plant is exhibiting curled leaves due to prolonged heat stress.

Wasps are hanging around my fruit plants and not letting me harvest. What can I do to move the insects to another location?

It's one of few things that we can be sure of every summer. Wasps will be hovering around the fruit we need to pick and, as often as not, eating it too. It's bad enough that we have to compete with birds for those sweet morsels, but at least they don't bite and sting!

During spring and early summer, wasps are major pollinators and predators, seeking protein from pollen and from the insects they prey upon. In this role, wasps are major benefactors of the garden. Most of the pollen and insects are brought back to feed the next generation of wasp larvae. In return, the larvae secrete a rich sugary carbohydrate to fuel all their work. It's a feedback loop, and the worker wasps are addicted to the sugar provided by the larvae, so they are motivated to feed and tend the growing wasps. But then things change. After two weeks or so, the larvae are ready to pupate, spinning a cocoon and no longer needing to be fed, and more to the point no longer secreting the sugar that the worker wasps want and need. They will return to flowers for pollen and nectar but will also be drawn to the smell of ripening fruit.[16]

They are hungry, and because wasps are territorial — like we are — they are prepared to fight for what they desire. It is a natural cycle, just like our desire for picnics and barbecues outdoors at the height of summer, and our desire not to be stung while enjoying them.

If we view (and we should) wasps as necessary for the health of the garden ecosystem, then we need to find ways to coexist that don't involve death for wasps or our pain and possible allergic reactions to their venom.

In spring, as the queen wasps seek to build a nest, watch for activity where wasps are zeroing in on a particular spot. If it is going to be a nest in a problematic location, destroy the nest before the queen has a chance to lay the first eggs, which will be the worker wasps. This is especially important if the nest is going to be in a fruit tree!

We often think of wasps as huge garden pests, but they actually have important roles in the ecosystem. (Photo courtesy of Tina Boisvert)

This action will prevent nearby encounters but won't prevent wasps visiting from the neighbours. Onward to the second line of defence; wasps have highly developed senses of smell, hence their being attracted to the aroma of fruit, and your pop can. They do not like sharp smells like basil, sage, and mint. Nor lavender for some reason. And they really dislike citrus. Make sprays from the herbs and peels and spray the trees and even the fruit as a repellent. Or use essential oils in sprays.

Measures that are largely ineffective include the paper nests meant to fool wasps that that piece of territory is taken. Wasps are smart. They know it is a fake. Wasp traps of any sort are also to be avoided as they will also attract other insects such as our native bees and indiscriminately kill them too. As the average wasp nest has worker wasps in the thousands, the chances of any wasp trap killing off sufficient numbers to turn the tide are slim at best. Plus, there is the distasteful job of dealing with the trap after it has its mass of decomposing bodies inside.

As large fruits start to mature, do enclose them in muslin bags to keep wasps from eating the fruit, especially if you previously had problems with wasps decimating the harvest.

Harvest early in the day when the wasps are still sleeping.

Make sure to clean up any windfall right away. Besides being messy, the fermenting fruit flesh is a magnet for wasps to come a-flying to feast.

Avoid planting fruit trees with soft succulent fruit, such as plums and apricots. Wasps can even tunnel into the fruit, and I once nearly bit one in half as I was eating a newly harvested, juicy plum. I am not sure I have recovered from the experience even at many years removed.

Apples and pears do not seem to offer the same draw, and the earlier-maturing berries are often ready to harvest before the wasps turn from feeding the larvae to having to fend for themselves.

Finally, develop as high a tolerance for wasps being drawn to your fruit as you possibly can. They are hungry and are almost at the end of their lives after working hard all summer. Even more to think on, the world needs wasps more than it needs us humans for the functions they perform in the balanced ecosystem.

But if the wasps need to go to protect you and your family, there are professionals that can remove nests both safely and without using broad-spectrum pesticides that will do immense damage to other wildlife in the garden.[17] —JM

How can I prevent birds from eating the berries from my haskaps, saskatoons, and goji plants?

I will never forget the time I was harvesting saskatoon berries and perched on the other side of the bush was a robin, busily eating them as fast as he or she could while I did the same. It wasn't moving, and neither was I, and we kept our beady eyes fixed on each other the whole time!

If my presence wasn't enough to deter that robin, then something more was needed. As always, I respect its need to eat, but then so do I. It was time to deploy some other means to ward off its deprivations if I was going to get enough for a pie.

So, what to do if you grow it but you don't get to eat it?

Forget scarecrows for starters. They are nice perching stations as far as I can see. Small shrubs can be easily covered with fairly close-weave cotton netting with small half-inch (1.25-centimetre) holes—larger holes may trap the heads of birds as they seek to get in. However, don't just lay it on top; rather, use supports so that it is held out from all the stems. Lightweight, floating row cover can be used too for smaller plants to great effect, especially if it is made into a portable cage.

Birds don't like noises and flashing lights they do not understand. Commercial orchards use big booming noisemakers, but that would likely irritate most neighbours and isn't necessary. You can buy Mylar bird scare tape and hang it from branches. Its shiny surfaces flash light, which scares off birds for as long as they haven't figured out that it isn't a danger. I like to go with old CDs and DVDs that aren't needed anymore. If they are placed closely together, not only do they flash but they clash and bash. I have used empty milk jugs, too, to some purpose. Likewise, pinwheels, pie plates, and Christmas decorations. A more aesthetic look can be chimes. But each works for only so long, until those birds get wise.

Then there are predator deterrents. Plastic or resin owls, mounted in a natural place for an owl, can be just the ticket. You can even get ones that move their wings and have built-in speakers. Effective but may be annoying after a while?

Some people advocate feeding birds so they aren't quite so hungry, but if you go that route the feeding station should be far enough away from the fruit trees and shrubs that the birds don't view them as dessert.

In the end, what we need to do to save our sanity is respect that those birds are hungry animals, just like us. As Ann Ralph says, "Just grow more fruit. That way they can't possibly get everything."[18] It seems to me to be good advice! —JM

This may appear to be a drastic measure, but if you want some of those delicious strawberries for yourself, keeping them away from birds is necessary.

It's early summer and my apple tree just lost a ton of fruit. What is going on?

This is called June drop. Don't panic when this happens; it's perfectly natural! If trees such as apples, plums, and pears get a bit too burdened with developing fruit, they take action to prevent all of it from maturing. Of course, that sounds silly to us at the outset, but do you really want copious amounts of tiny, overcrowded fruits that might not taste as good as they should? Or run the risk of branches breaking under the stress of so much bounty? Nope. So, the tree thins itself.[19] —SN

Why aren't my apple trees bearing fruit this year? How can I improve the chances of good yield in all my fruit plants?

There are myriad variables at play every year that affect how our apple and other fruit trees and shrubs bear fruit. It's hard to pinpoint any one factor when they have a poor year.

There are around six major reasons for little to no fruit and a bunch of minor ones too.

The first is age. If your tree is young, it may not have reached the age that it will bear fruit reliably. Many of the saplings we buy are on dwarf rootstock, which results in flowering and fruit up to five years earlier than if the tree is on seedling rootstock.[20] But the tree still needs to be mature enough to have the energy to do both. If you have been noticing a decline in fruit production over a few years, then the tree may simply be at the age that it says enough is enough and goes into retirement.

The next big category is the environmental conditions, such as the health of the soil, nutrient availability, and whether the soil has decent moisture retention. Compost provided annually as a top dressing to improve soil structure and texture and provide nutrients will go a long way toward eliminating that consideration. Review your watering regime as well—most trees require water only when the soil is dry rather than on a specific schedule. When watering, ensure the amount is sufficient to soak the entire soil profile rather than a shallow application. But overwatering is just as bad, promoting conditions for rot. If you are providing additional fertilizer, be aware that a fertilizer high in nitrogen will promote foliage growth at the expense of flowering. While doing your assessment, also check that the tree is still receiving enough sunlight. Are other trees overshadowing or crowding it? There may have been enough sun before but new buildings going up or a maturing garden can really affect that vital requirement. While you are at it, check that neither grass nor weeds have encroached into the drip line zone and are competing for resources.

How we train and prune our trees also affects production. If the tree has not been pruned for a while, there may be dead, diseased branches impeding the health of the tree. Crossing branches and generally dense canopy will need to be thinned out to allow in air and sunlight. On the other hand, if it was pruned last year it may need to recover this year, or if overpruned, unfortunately, the tree may be concentrating on growing new branches and leaves at the expense of fruiting. We recommend having an arborist visit to help train fruit trees unless you are knowledgeable as incorrect pruning can take a long time to remediate.

An arborist can also inspect the tree to determine if it has picked up a disease or is infested by insects and can provide recommendations for courses of action. If you see lots of ants on the tree, look for aphids too, and that is a sign of something being wrong with the health of the tree. Time to call in the experts.

Our apple trees and most of the rest of our fruit trees and shrubs need insects for pollination. We can all use more of them in the garden, so check to see if your other plants are those that will invite them in, be it for food, water, or shelter. Boosting biodiversity in your garden will go a long way toward ensuring enough pollinators are around to get to work in the first place.

Apples and other fruit trees that require cross-pollination will need a companion of a different variety within fifty to one hundred feet (fifteen to thirty metres), one that blooms at the same time. We often do not need to worry about cross-pollination in the city given the preponderance of crabapples in gardens, but perhaps the one that was the cross-pollinator in previous years is no longer there? It is best to have your own second variety on your property!

Did the tree have a bumper crop last year? If so, this year is a rest year as it doesn't have enough energy to flower and develop fruit. It is called biennial bearing, and those lean years after a prolific year are down to the trees beginning the process of flower formation for next season right after this year's crop matures. Sometimes there is little energy left for anything but a few sparse flowers the following year. It is best in a heavy fruit-setting year to thin out the crop after June to one fruit every ten inches (twenty-five centimetres) instead of clumps of three or more fruit on a single spur. This applies to pears, plums, and apricots too, except that they can be a little closer together. It hurts to do it, but the result will be fruit that is larger and tastier and consistent from year to year.

Then there is the really big one: our weather!

This apple tree is flowering spectacularly, but that's not the only thing that must go right for a massive crop of fruit.

Cold snaps at the wrong time can seriously damage flower buds and even immature fruit, causing them to die. In 2022, in Calgary, we had a really warm period in early February followed by a quick drop of temperatures to −13°F (−25°C). Some trees had already started to come out of dormancy, and some were even starting to bud out. We saw major damage to all those buds and many had very few fruits to harvest. When trees are flowering, even temperatures just below the freezing mark will cause some damage to petals and/or styles, and you can be sure that if we have a few nights of 25°F (−4°C) after flowering begins, we are in trouble. Throw in some chilling north winds with some windchill and it gets worse.

Pollinator activity when it is cold and wet also drops off considerably. Most bees are fair-weather insects and huddle in the bunker when weather turns nasty, but the flowers are out there no matter what and don't hang around forever.

Heat and drought can affect our trees too, and especially a dry spring with little ground moisture to start with can affect flowering at the outset. Wildfire smoke and urban pollution can also affect flowering and subsequent fruit formation. In the fall, drought can affect fruit bud formation.

On the other hand, a mild fall and winter may mean trees do not go into dormancy properly and thus, come spring, are slow to bud out with all the problems that delay can bring.[21] It seems a thought ridiculous for the Great White North, but our climate is moderating and the seasons with it.

Considering all the variables that can affect our trees' ability to flower, get pollinated, and then develop fruit, it seems a minor miracle every season when we can rejoice to see the bounty developing before our eyes. But it does happen, and all we can do is take advantage of every opportunity to promote the health and welfare of our fruit trees and shrubs so that they can perform that miracle.[22]—JM

I have a hardy apricot tree, but it never bears any fruit. Why not?

One thing to know before you slap down your credit card at the garden centre on a beautiful new hardy apricot tree: you may not get fruit from it very often. It's not that they aren't excellent producers—the issue is that they bloom extremely early in the spring, and here on the prairies, we quite often get a late hard frost that completely does the little flowers in. No flowers = no fruit. Fortunately, apricots are gorgeous trees and well suited to many of our landscapes, and you won't *always* be thwarted by frost. Some years, you'll get to enjoy those tasty fruits.—SN

When I cut open my apple fruits, they have clear, watery patches inside. What causes this?

This interesting issue is called water core, and it's not due to any sort of pathogen or pest. Water core usually occurs just before the apples are harvested, and you'll see it most often in fruit that was harvested late (meaning it sat on the tree longer than it needed to). Water core is sometimes caused by irregular watering, but it can also be caused by weather conditions, such as a prolonged sequence of hot days and chilly nights.

Taken all at once, these types of issues are usually brought on by prolonged dry and hot weather. As gardeners, we all long to control the weather, but we can't, so we have to make do with trying to manage the stress of our plants and help them along through the worst of the elements. In this case, keep up with a regular watering schedule, and go extremely easy on—or altogether avoid—the fertilizer. I know, it's your gut reaction to give the plants more nutrients when they look sad, but unless your soil is really deficient, you'll want to hold off. If you haven't already applied mulch to the base of the trees or shrubs, do so now (see pages 28–29 for tips on how to do this). Watch closely for signs of other issues, such as insects and pests, and use appropriate controls or treatments for the problems if they arise. Beyond this, don't fret—if the weather co-operates the following year, the plant should rebound. You can safely eat apples that have water core (some people say it actually makes them taste sweeter), but they lack the capability for long-term storage.[23]—sn

Water core is ugly but there's no need to chuck the affected fruit into the compost bin.

My cherry fruit is bursting open before the cherries are fully ripe. What is going on?

If you're just getting ready for what promises to be a glorious harvest of sour cherries and the fruit starts cracking just as the cherries are nearing ripeness, it can be disappointing. Cherry cracking sometimes takes place due to the change in the amounts of sugars in the ripening fruit, combined with an unfortunately timed rainfall or even a sudden period of high humidity. What happens is moisture accumulates where the cuticle (outer layer) of the fruit is at its thinnest, which is that shallow depression at the top of the fruit, where the stem is attached. The scenario goes something like this: the cherries are gathering sugars, they are growing extremely quickly, and then—bam!—a tiny puddle of water sits for a prolonged period in that depression and causes the cuticle to start to form tiny cracks. As the fruit swells with the intake of water, the sides might split.

Cherry cracking may also occur when the ground is saturated with too much water. This is something the gardener can control to a certain extent. Watch how much supplemental irrigation you offer.[24]—SN

Almost ready to pick! This is the time when cracking is most likely to occur.

Why do blueberries and haskaps have dusty-looking greyish blotches on the fruit skin? Does this mean they are diseased?

This is called a bloom, and it isn't an indicator that something is wrong with the fruit—in fact, it's kind of a good thing that it's there! A fruit's bloom is actually a natural waxy, protective coating used to keep the fruit from being exposed to problems such as insect attacks or bacteria. The bloom also keeps the fruit from desiccating quickly. Not all berries or fruit of the same species are going to have a bloom, so if you don't see one on your haskaps or plums, it's all good. And you should be doing a proper job of washing your fruits and berries anyway, but you don't need to spend extra time scrubbing off the bloom, as it's perfectly safe to eat.[25]—SN

How can I minimize hail damage to my fruit plants?

Hailstorms are an unwelcome but extremely common part of prairie living, and they can do severe damage to our gardens and our homes. When it comes to fruit plants, hail can injure plant tissues on leaves, flowers, stems, and branches, and ruin developing or unharvested fruit. The wounds caused by the icy stones can invite pathogens such as fungi and bacteria. Most home gardeners can do nothing after a storm but clean up the damage and hope their wounded trees rebound—and that they get some kind of harvest out of their plants. Pruning broken branches and thinning affected fruit can also help the plants on their road to recovery. Keeping up with regular maintenance and care such as watering and fertilizing is also important following a devastating storm.

The key to preventing all of this is to try to take action before the inevitable strikes. If you are growing a lot of fruit plants, investing in hail netting—despite its huge expense—can be extremely worthwhile. Some gardeners will erect barriers made from hardware cloth if they live in a hail-prone region.

You can use heavy-duty row cover fabric with shrubs, although it offers virtually no aesthetic value. If you choose to use row cover fabric, you will need hoops or stakes to keep it up off the plants. Use white covers so that they don't contribute to heat stress. These would presumably be a short-term solution, used on the day that you expect a storm. Other short-term solutions include erecting temporary tents made from burlap, tarps, and even bedsheets. No matter what you use, keep the fabric from touching the branches and stems as much as possible and stake the cloth down so that it doesn't blow away.[26]—SN

Hail can seriously injure your plants. The white substance you see on the stems of the plant in this photo is mildew, a secondary issue for the stressed plant.

Fruitful Thinking

What are some native fruit-bearing shrubs I can grow in my garden?

It is natural that gardeners gravitate to apples, pears, cherries, and plums, not to mention strawberries and blueberries. They are the fruit we grow up with and enjoy.

However, for the most part, they originate from climates quite different than ours. They may not be fully hardy, require more water than usually falls as rain, and are subject to pests that they may not have defences built in to naturally combat.

It is striking that the prairies did not have fruit trees when they were settled by Europeans, and it is only through breeding programs that we now have species that are successful for our climate.

What does grow in profusion are shrubs and ground covers that Indigenous people took full advantage of in their diet. They are perfectly suited to both the climate and the growing conditions of the prairies. While some are not suited to a cultivated garden—as they quickly spread and overcome the garden—others are delightful in our gardens.

Some species are well known to us, and there are both the species and hybrids available to us. Saskatoons, also known as Juneberry and serviceberry, have a huge native range. Blueberries are native across Canada with distinct zones for various species. We can grow our native lowbush species or cultivars that are both well known and successful.

Cultivated haskaps (*Lonicera caerulea*), bred from a species originating in Japan (*Lonicera caerulea* var. *emphyllocalyx*), are the subject of an extensive breeding program at the University of Saskatchewan. The species is to be found on the edges of our boreal forests.

While we grow cultivars of gooseberries and raspberries, they too are both native to the prairies. Golden currant (*Ribes aureum*) is native across Canada and resides in my garden where I enjoy its black berries. But there are also native blackcurrants to be found, such as *Ribes americanum*, northern blackcurrant (*Ribes hudsonianum*), and prickly currant (*Ribes lacustre*). Northern redcurrant (*Ribes triste*) is native

Sea buckthorn is an aggressive spreader often grown as erosion control, but it also produces delicious citrus-flavoured berries.

to northern Saskatchewan and Manitoba. There are several native gooseberries, such as sticky gooseberry (*Ribes lobbii*), white-stemmed gooseberry (*Ribes inerme*), and northern gooseberry (*Ribes oxyacanthoides*). While I love my 'Heritage' raspberry bushes, do check out our native species with their tinier flavour bombs, such as red raspberry (*Rubus idaeus*), Arctic raspberry (*Rubus arcticus*), trailing raspberry (*Rubus pubescens*), and creeping raspberry (*Rubus pedatus*) that makes such a great ground cover. We have native strawberries too, with wild strawberry (*Fragaria virginiana*) and wood strawberry (*Fragaria vesca*) to be readily found.

Sea buckthorn (*Hippophae rhamnoides*) has lately been recognized for its bright orange berries that are loaded with vitamin C. (Do check whether it is on an invasive species list for your area before purchasing.) Likewise highbush cranberry (*Viburnum trilobum*) has long been grown as an ornamental shrub, but its astringent fruit can be most valuable. Chokecherry (*Prunus virginiana*) is also native but comes with the warning that the flesh must be cooked to be safe.

Other native shrubs may be too aggressive in an urban garden, but if there is enough space for the plants to colonize and form thickets, then silver buffalo berry (*Shepherdia argentea*) and Canada buffalo berry (*Shepherdia canadensis*) have delicious berries, with Canada buffalo berry being the tarter of the two. Both need full sun and well-drained soil to thrive, but cloudberry (*Rubus chamaemorus*) with its salmon-coloured berries needs the opposite as it prefers peaty bogs and shade. Its cousin thimbleberry (*Rubus parviflorus*) is a species of the montane ecosystem (mountain slopes) and thrives in shade. Its berries have a neutral taste, but it boasts magnificent maple-like leaves.

We tend not to think of fruit being a ground cover, but Oregon grape (*Mahonia repens*), common bearberry (*Arctostaphylos uva-ursi*), and alpine bearberry (*Arctous alpina*) all have edible fruit. They prefer sandy soils in full sun. Just do not eat them in any quantity as too many may cause adverse reactions. Ramblers that grow in shade are fairybells, with Hooker's fairybells (*Prosartes hookeri*) and rough-fruited fairybells (*Prosartes trachycarpa*) both providing sweet treats.

Including native species of fruit is a great way to broaden the biodiversity in our gardens, besides being good eating. Ensure that the place where you want to locate them matches, as close as possible, their native habitat to promote success and provide the appropriate space for any that love to form thickets.[1] —JM

Bearberry (also known as kinnikinnick) is an interesting native fruit plant that may be a wonderful addition to your garden!

What are a few unusual fruit plants to consider for my prairie garden?

We love our common fruits, from apples to cherries, strawberries to currants, but there are many more species we can look to grow that are just that bit more exotic or unfamiliar, at least to most of us. Sometimes that unusual fruit is a newly bred hybrid or a variety that is now making its way to the garden nurseries. Some are species that we didn't imagine we could grow.

Many are borderline hardy for the prairies, though the eastern prairies will have much different growing conditions than the high altitudes near the Rockies. Southern portions have a longer growing season than up north bordering the territories. But others are just as hardy as the ones we usually have in our gardens.

Then there is our ever-changing weather and climate. What we can grow now used to be completely out of scope not that long ago. Perhaps not today but soon?

Top of the category of "been around for a while, but we have only now noticed them" is the pink blueberry (*Vaccinium corymbosum* 'Pink Lemonade'). It features silver-green foliage and bright pink berries that the birds don't go after because they think they are not ripe. More for us, and they do have a flavour of their namesake.

Goji berry (*Lycium barbarum*), also known as wolfberry, native to east Asia, is becoming more and more common. It belongs to the tomato family (Solanaceae) and grows into thickets some three to six feet (one to two metres) high. The drop-shaped red fruit is considered a superfood in some circles and is sweeter than most fruit we grow on the prairies. It does need to be kept in check, so keep an eye on it starting to spread once well established.

Another berry to perhaps consider is tayberry (*Rubus fruticosus* × *R. idaeus*), named after the River Tay in Scotland. It is a cross between blackberry and red raspberry. For those of us who find blackberry to be somewhat dodgy to overwinter, tayberry has that extra bit of hardiness. Not only that, but the canes are thornless, with berries that have the dark purple colour we love to love.

Goji berry shrubs have lovely delicate flowers
followed by (usually copious) quantities of
delicious red fruit.

If not tayberry, then how about lingonberry (*Vaccinium vitis-idaea*), also known as cowberry, which is a relative of blueberry and cranberry? I always associated lingonberry with Scandinavia, but it has been determined that it is native to North America too as a subspecies (*V. vitis-idaea* subsp. *minus*), which is much shorter with smaller red fruit than its European cousins. There are several cultivars that have been bred from the larger European species on the market. Another relative of blueberry is the red huckleberry (*Vaccinium parvifolium*), also known as red bilberry. Native to the west coast of North America from Alaska down to northern California, it is considered hardy to USDA zone 5, roughly equivalent to the Canadian rating of zone 4. This one is a shade lover and wants the soils usually found in woodland settings. Its native habitat is quite different from our usual prairie soils and climate, but as with blueberries, if one has just the right spot, it is a possibility. The small berries are salmon coloured and are a great alternative to any of the currants.

Love kiwi? Then hardy kiwi (*Actinidia arguta*) and variegated-leaf kiwi, also known as Arctic kiwi (*A. kolomikta*), relatives of the fuzzy brown fruit we adore, are vines to love. The grape-sized fruit doesn't get peeled; they just pop into your mouth whole. Arctic Beauty (*A. kolomikta* 'Arctic Beauty') with its variegated white, green, and pink foliage is a stunner but requires male and female plants for pollination. Consider Issai (*A. arguta* 'Issai') if you wish a self-pollinating cultivar.

Just consider the possibilities![2] —JM

Which fruit plants can be grown as hedges?

Hedges are usually grown to demarcate boundaries, as privacy barriers, as wind-breaks, or as wildlife habitat. Typically, hedges are composed of evergreen or deciduous woody ornamentals, but why not have your hedge and eat it, too?

Bear in mind that if your hedge separates your property line from your neighbour's, minimal fruit litter is likely to be appreciated, so you'll want to select plants that aren't too messy or ensure you take the time and effort to do the necessary cleanup. As well, if you need to prune the hedge regularly (I'm looking at you, raspberries!), be a courteous and diligent neighbour and keep up with the task. When planning out your hedge, it's a good idea to discuss your ideas for plant selections with your neighbours. (It probably wouldn't hurt to share the fruit, as well!) Do your research before you buy to check for characteristics such as growth habit, size, type of spread, thorniness, and so on. Here are a few selections to try as hedges in your prairie garden:

* Chokeberry (*Aronia melanocarpa*)
* Currant (*Ribes odoratum, R. aureum, R. rubrum*)
* Gooseberry (*Ribes uva-crispa, R. hirtellum*)
* Haskap (*Lonicera caerulea*)
* Highbush cranberry (*Viburnum trilobum*)
* Nanking cherry (*Prunus tomentosa*)
* Raspberry (*Rubus idaeus*)
* Rose, prickly (*Rosa acicularis*)
* Saskatoon (*Amelanchier alnifolia*)—**SN**

Edible hedge? Yes, please! Gooseberries are a good option.

Can I grow watermelon on the prairies? If so, how?

Yes, you absolutely can grow watermelon on the prairies, and cantaloupe, honeydew, and other melons as well! The key is to manage your expectations: these are fruits that need a long, warm growing season to be able to grow and ripen on the plant. (No, watermelons do not continue to ripen after picking.) You will not be growing watermelon fruit of the respectable girth that can feed entire sports teams. Your garden watermelons will be small, but sweeter than any you've ever tasted in your life. When buying your seeds, look for miniature watermelons with the shortest days to maturity that you can find: 'Sugar Baby' is a good recommendation at eighty days, as is 'Black Beauty'. Bear in mind that not all watermelons are pink inside—the beautiful heirloom 'Cream of Saskatchewan' is yellow white and matures in eighty to eighty-five days.

If you have a greenhouse, grow your watermelons in it and give them plenty of space in a large container. They will sprawl everywhere; this is not a plant for small-space gardeners. If you need to grow them outside, start them indoors in March and transplant them if the weather is co-operative in early June. Give them well-drained soil with compost mixed in, and keep the plants well watered throughout the growing season. If your weather co-operates and you get a sufficient amount (and by that I mean three months!) of warmth, you will hopefully have watermelon fruit ripening at the end of August or early September, just before the first frost.[3] —SN

Who wouldn't want to try growing this beauty? Waiting patiently until 'Cream of Saskatchewan' watermelon is ready to harvest and eat is the hard part!

I hear that ground cherries take a long time to mature. Can we grow them successfully on the prairies?

Ground cherries (*Physalis pruinosa* and *P. peruviana*) are members of the nightshade family and bear small, sweet, yellow-orange fruit wrapped in husks. The most popular and easy-to-source variety is the heirloom 'Aunt Molly's'. Ground cherries take about seventy to seventy-five days to mature once transplanted into the garden, so with our short growing season on the prairies, it helps to start the seeds indoors before the decent spring weather arrives outside. Get them going in late March, for transplanting out in early June. (This timing takes into account the fact that the seeds need up to two weeks to germinate.)

Like their relatives, tomatoes and tomatillos, ground cherries love the heat, so for optimum success, give them a full-sun location. Water them consistently and regularly. Ground cherries can be easily grown in a raised bed (in fact, that may be preferable if your soil is predominantly clay-based, as the plants require excellent drainage).

Ground cherries tend to sprawl a little bit, but if you're concerned about the space they take up, you can confine them to tomato cages. Mulch the base of the plants with straw to help conserve soil moisture and maintain even soil temperatures. These plants do not care for cool, wet summers, so don't blame yourself if it's been one of those years and your ground cherry plants have not produced abundantly. You've increased your chances at a harvest by starting your plants indoors and giving them sufficient time to mature, so hopefully your efforts will be rewarded.[4] —SN

When talking about strawberries, what do we mean by June-bearing, everbearing, and day-neutral varieties?

Picture this: You're standing in an aisle of a greenhouse, trying to figure out which strawberry plant to buy. The pots are full of attractive leaves, and the plants all look pretty much the same right now, so—simply going by the information on the labels—how the heck do you know which ones are going to produce the most abundant fruit, at the time you want them to?

Fruitful strawberry production (pun intended) comes down to day length. (As the term suggests, that is a measure of how many hours of daylight and darkness occur in a twenty-four-hour period as the seasons progress, as well as the corresponding temperature changes.) June-bearing strawberries produce flower buds during the late summer and autumn of the previous year, as the day length begins to shorten, then they bloom in spring. A crop of early strawberry fruit pops up as the days grow longer in June (sometimes early July on the prairies). They yield only one large burst of delicious fruit each year, and they produce copious runners so you can keep on growing more plants over the long term.

Day length dictates bountiful strawberry harvests.

Everbearing strawberries produce fruit in late June or early July and keep doing so until early autumn. The fruit is often smaller than that of June-bearing or day-neutral types, and you get the benefit of a longer period for picking. They don't produce a ton of runners like June-bearers do.

Day-neutral strawberry varieties were developed from everbearing breeding stock and will usually produce more fruit than everbearing types. They don't really respond to day length in quite the same way as June-bearing or everbearing varieties (that's where the "day-neutral" part comes in), and they will set flower buds all growing season unless the temperatures soar. They will usually produce two main crops a year, in late June or early July, then again in August until the first frost. They usually completely stall out in the heat of the summer, but if the weather is cooler, you might get a few extra harvests outside the two main fruiting periods.

On the prairies, if you want to grow June-bearing strawberries, look for varieties such as 'Kent' and 'Bounty'. Decent everbearing strawberries for our climate include 'Fort Laramie' and 'Ogallala'. And if you're keen on day-neutrals, 'Tristar' and 'Seascape' are long-held favourites.[5] —sn

Cultivated blueberries seem to be difficult to grow in prairie gardens, but I really want to give them a shot! How can I improve my chances of success?

Ah, blueberries! Round, dark blue morsels of sweetness that have high levels of antioxidants that we can't get enough of in their short season.

There are eighteen or so species of blueberries (*Vaccinium* spp.) native to Canada, and Indigenous peoples have been harvesting them for food and medicinal uses for centuries. Not only that, but wild blueberries have been managed by both First Nations and settlers by selective burning of the stands to encourage vigorous growth and production.[6] The practice of management of wild blueberries continues, but commercial production of the fruit is enormous.

The lowbush blueberry (*V. angustifolium*) is largely found from Manitoba through to the Atlantic provinces down into the United States. Less hardy for our climate, the highbush blueberry (*V. corymbosum*) and its cultivars grow to six feet (two metres) and are the ones that account for most commercial production. Hardy lowbush blueberries that are native to the prairies include the velvetleaf blueberry (*V. myrtilloides*), dwarf blueberry (*V. caespitosum*), bog blueberry (*V. uliginosum*), and oval-leaf blueberry (*V. ovalifolium*).

Thankfully for gardeners, work has been ongoing since the early 1900s to hybridize hardy low-growing blueberries that have tiny fruit with the less hardy highbush species that are much taller and have bigger and more plentiful fruit. The result has been the half-high blueberries, which grow to around three feet (one metre) and which we largely see for sale to gardeners. Any cultivar with 'North' in its name, along with 'Chippewa', 'Polaris', and 'St. Cloud', is hardy enough to withstand our climate!

So, we have the cultivars that work for our world, but typically what we don't have is the soil. Blueberries, just like their cousins azalea and rhododendron, require acidic soil in the range of 4.5 to 5 pH. Our alkaline soils generally impair blueberry plants from taking up nutrients, resulting in chlorotic leaves and early death. Blueberries also require consistently moist—but not boggy—soils. They are self-pollinators, but having more than one plant, preferably of different cultivars, will aid in pollination and boost berry production too.

The key to success is to amend the soil where your plants will be to ensure it is acidic. Before you start, do a soil test to see where you are starting from pH-wise. Then incorporate into the soil large amounts of peat moss, which will both lower the pH and create the moisture retentive soil conditions to boot. If your original pH is over 7, then you will also need to add in elemental sulphur, iron sulphate, and/or aluminum sulphate, which will be converted by soil microbes over time to become sulphuric acid that will act to lower your soil's pH. Continue to do soil tests util your pH is at the ideal level and *then* plant. It may take a year to get your soil in the right condition, so pre-preparation is a great way to go.

Because I believe that our alkaline soils will fight tooth and nail being acidified, do take annual soil tests near where your blueberries are growing and continue to amend the soil whenever you see that pH creeping up again.

Blueberries are shallow-rooted plants, so mulch is essential to protect their roots from encroaching weeds and to maintain soil moisture. When fertilizing your plants, use organic fertilizers that will continue to maintain the acidity of the soil. If you are having trouble maintaining that pH, use aluminum sulphate as a fertilizer as it contains nitrogen as well.

Then watch them grow![7] —JM

What fruit or parts of fruit plants are poisonous?

We are all a little leery of fruit that we are not sure is safe to eat. After all, Snow White was given a poisoned apple by the Wicked Stepmother. We have grown up with the knowledge that red means danger, but does it apply to fruit? Or are black, purple, white, or even green also potentially deadly?

Certainly, the green fruit of potatoes is to be avoided. It is loaded with solanine, a glycoalkaloid, and can be deadly. Tomatoes, when first introduced to the Old World from Mexico, were considered to be "poison apples." They were novel and expensive, and only the nobility could afford or even have access to them. Problem was the acid in tomatoes reacted with the lead in the pewter dishes that such wealthy people could afford, and the result was lead poisoning. Easy to blame the poor red tomato because it also belongs to the nightshade family (Solanaceae), as does deadly nightshade. Not to mention that Gerard's *Herball*, published in 1597, had a very low opinion of them.

Other berries that are red and poisonous to us include baneberry (*Actaea rubra*), red elder (*Sambucus pubens*), yew (*Taxus* spp.), and cotoneaster (*Cotoneaster* spp.). Count the bright red berries of asparagus (*Asparagus officinalis*) among them, not that we usually consider them fruit we would munch on.

The fruits that we generally cultivate carry hidden dangers too. Not the flesh, but the seeds, stones, and pits. Apricot stones contain amygdalin, a toxic cyanogenic glycoside. Products containing ground-up apricot stones, such as exfoliating creams, have been pulled from the market before now because of the danger. Likewise, cherries, Nanking cherries, plums, peaches, and nectarines, being members of the same genus (*Prunus*), have the same properties. So don't crunch on that cherry pit, as it will release hydrogen cyanide. Apples and pears too, but a few seeds crunched inadvertently will not be a problem.

Chokecherries are not named "choke" for nothing. It's not because of the taste of the fruit—though I find it bitter—it's because of the stones, which contain hydrocyanic acid. They will make you choke for sure, permanently.

120

Interestingly, our native animals know which fruits need to have the seeds and pits spit out, be they chipmunks or birds. Deer know to avoid them altogether. It is our pets, livestock, and us—notably our children—that do not have that innate knowledge and get into trouble.

So, if you do not know for sure if the fruit on any plant is safe, don't eat it, and avoid munching on the seeds, pits, and stones regardless![8]—JM

Chokecherries contain stones that should not be eaten.

When is it time to harvest my fruit plants?

FRUIT	READY TO HARVEST
Apples and crabapples	When you cut a fruit in half and the seeds have turned black; when the fruit is the colour it is supposed to be for that variety at the time of the season it is to be picked
Apricots	When plump and full of juice
Cherries, ground	When they have fallen to the ground
Cherries, sour	When the fruit is shiny, full colour (not pale), soft to the touch
Chokecherries	When the fruit is in full colour and just soft to the touch

How can I store and use them?

HOW TO PICK	STORAGE AND USES
Hold apple and give it a gentle twist; should come away easily from tree	Fresh—eat right away or wrap individual apples in newspaper and store in boxes in cool, dry conditions Baking, cooking Preserves Juice, cider Freezing (cooked or raw) Dehydrated
Pick manually, should be easy to remove from stems	Fresh eating Baking Preserves Juice Freezing (remove stones) Dehydrated
Collect them from the ground, remove papery husks	Fresh eating Baking Preserves Freezing
Pick manually; if the fruit is ripe, the stems will easily come away from the plant	Fresh eating Baking Preserves Juice Freezing (remove pits) Dehydrated
Cut the clusters off with scissors and separate the berries by hand	Fresh Baking Preserves Freezing

FRUIT	READY TO HARVEST
Currants	When in full colour; when berry is firm
Gooseberries	When plump and fully green or red (depending on variety)
Grapes	When plump, firm to the touch, full of juice, and full colour for variety
Haskap	When full colour (not green or red, but dark purple blue), juicy
Pears	When nearly ripe, still a bit firm to the touch; in full colour; if eating fresh, wait until they are ripe and soft on tree
Plums	When firm and full colour
Pumpkins, winter squash	When full colour and size; when rind is firm; should sound hollow when tapped (can ripen off plant if necessary)

HOW TO PICK	STORAGE AND USES
Cut strigs (fruit clusters) off with scissors, then separate each berry by hand; snip off the tips of the berries	Fresh Baking Preserves Juice, wine Freezing
Pick by hand, trim tips off	Fresh eating Baking Preserves Freezing
Pick clusters by hand	Fresh eating Baking Preserves Juice, wine Freezing
Pick by hand (berries are very soft so be careful)	Fresh eating Baking Preserves Freezing Dehydrated
Hold in hand and gently twist away from the tree	Fresh eating Baking, cooking Preserves Juice, perry Freezing (after poaching) Dehydrated
Hold in hand and gently twist away from the tree	Fresh eating Baking, cooking Preserves Freezing
Cut stem from plant with shears, leave six inches (fifteen centimetres) of stem on the fruit	Baking, cooking Preserves Freezing (roasted, puréed first)

FRUIT	READY TO HARVEST
Raspberries, red	When slightly firm, full red (not pale)
Saskatoons	When just softening, not hard; full dark purple (not red or green)
Sea buckthorn berries	When juicy and bright orange yellow
Strawberries	When slightly firm, not squishy; full red colour (no white or green patches)
Watermelon	When the underside of the melon (the part on the ground) turns pale yellow; when the melon rind is firm and loses its shiny gloss at the top near the stem

HOW TO PICK	STORAGE AND USES
Pick by hand, gently pull fruit away from receptacle	Fresh eating Baking, cooking Preserves Freezing
Pick by hand	Fresh eating Baking, cooking Preserves Freezing Dehydrated
Pick by hand (but be careful as they are difficult to remove from plant)	Fresh eating (be mindful of hard seeds) Baking, cooking Preserves Freezing Dehydrated
Pick by hand; remove stems and hull if desired	Fresh eating Baking, cooking Preserves Juice Freezing (sugar or without) Dehydrated
Cut stem from plant with shears; leave a minimum of two inches (five centimetres) of stem on the fruit (more is better)	Fresh eating Preserves Juice[9]

—SN

These apples are not yet ready to be picked. This variety isn't bright green when the fruit is ripe, but rather features a red blush.

These Ure pears are ready to be picked!

Pear fruits will continue to ripen after they are picked.

Which fruits continue to ripen after picking?

Bananas continue to ripen once they come home, but apples and oranges do not. Avocados don't even begin to ripen until after they are picked.

But how to definitively know which type of fruit will continue to ripen or not?

It all comes down to fruit falling into two categories—climacteric and non-climacteric—with climacteric fruit continuing to ripen after harvest, whereas the non-climacteric ones just sit there and become compost while you wait.

The key is the climacteric phase of maturing fruit. In climacteric fruit, the concentration of ethylene rapidly increases, which breaks down chlorophyll, triggers the conversion of starches to sugars, and ripens fruit quickly, only ceasing to be produced when the fruit is consumed. In non-climacteric fruit, ethylene is present but doesn't increase rapidly, with the fruit slowly maturing. Once the fruit is harvested ethylene is no longer produced.

Climacteric fruits include those bananas, but also apples, pears, peaches, cherries, plums, apricots, and tomatoes, among many others. Non-climacteric fruits are most berries, all squash, citrus, and oddly enough eggplant and peppers even though they are in the same family as tomatoes. Avocados are climacteric, but the trigger for ethylene rapid production is after being picked. They always seem to be the oddball!

Non-climacteric fruits can continue to ripen after being picked if they are in close proximity to climacteric fruit, hence the age-old trick of placing a banana with other fruit to hasten the process.

Modern-day harvesting often means that fruit is picked well before it is ripe, as it ships better when hard, and then close to arrival at its destination is exposed to ethylene to trigger the ripening process. The sacrifice is often colour and taste.

So, if you have the means and opportunity to allow your fruit to be close to or fully ripe on the plant before harvesting, then you have maximum taste, nutrition, and colour from your fruit.[10] —JM

It is hard to imagine our edible landscape without fruit. What a dreary world it would be without crisp apples, tart sour cherries, or delectable strawberries. The old saying that the fruits of our labour are always sweet truly applies to growing your own fruit!

Acknowledgements

From Janet and Sheryl:

We've met so many gardeners of diverse experiences and backgrounds as we've been writing these books, and we are immensely grateful for their feedback and reactions to the series. Thank you to everyone who has supported and encouraged us on our journey! We've had many people ask us for more information about edible gardening, so we hope this particular book is useful to all of you!

Many thanks to Tina Boisvert, who generously contributed a photograph to the book.

There is no way to sufficiently express how thankful and appreciative we are for the entire publishing team at TouchWood Editions—it's such an absolute dream to work with all of you! We're now a few years into this series and we still can't believe it's all real! Thank you also to Tree Abraham for the fabulous cover illustrations and design.

From Janet:

What a fruitful and supportive partnership we have, Sheryl! Such a delight to be writing these books alongside you these past few years! So many thanks to all the pioneers of fruit-growing on the prairies, past and present. Our gardens wouldn't be the same without all the work that has gone into breeding fruit varieties that are hardy for us. As always, special gratitude to Steve, Jennifer, and David, not to mention the cats, for all that you do every day!

From Sheryl:

Immense gratitude and love to Rob and Mum and Dad and Derek. And serious props to Janet, who is absolutely the best co-author I could ever ask for!

Notes

Introduction

1. Britannica (website), "Fruit."

2. Kelly, "What Is a Fruit?," New York Botanical Garden (website).

3. Harvey, "What's the Difference between Fruit and Vegetables?," Live Science (website).

4. Kington, "Miles Kington Quotes," Goodreads (website).

Chapter One

1. Britannica (website), "Fruit"; Armstrong, "Identification of Major Fruit Types," palomar.edu; A. Grant, "Understanding Different Fruit Types," Gardening Know How (website).

2. A. Grant, "Fruit Bearing Shade Plants: Growing Fruiting Plants for Shade Gardens," Gardening Know How (website); Huffstetler, "Fruits That Grow in the Shade," The Spruce (website); Brown and Elsner, "Considerations for Growing Backyard Tree Fruit," Michigan State University (website).

3. Williams and Bors, *Growing Fruit in Northern Gardens*, 36–40; BioAdvanced (website), "Growing Trees: Bare-Root Advantages and Timing"; Poizner, "Why Buy a Young Whip If There Are Large Fruit Trees for Sale?," Orchard People (website).

4. Williams and Bors, *Growing Fruit in Northern Gardens*, 18–21.

5. Ralph, *Grow a Little Fruit Tree*, 40–41, 71–72.

6. Williams and Bors, *Growing Fruit in Northern Gardens*, 199–201.

7. Deardorff and Wadsworth, *What's Wrong with My Fruit Garden?*, 28–29; Deep Green Permaculture (website), "Backyard Orchard Culture, a New Approach to Growing Fruit in Limited Spaces."

8. Gardener's Supply Company (website), "Growing Berries and Asparagus in Raised Beds"; Saleem, "How to Grow Blueberries in a Raised Bed?," Bed-Gardening (website); Epic Gardening (website), "Raspberry Raised Bed Tips: Getting Things Growing."

9. Cloud Mountain Farm Center (website), "Encouraging Pollinators in Your Orchard and Garden"; McGinnis, "Smart Gardening: Pollination in Vegetable

Gardens and Backyard Fruit," Michigan State University (website); Byrne and Wojcik, "Selecting Plants for Pollinators," Pollinator Partnership Canada (website).

Chapter Two

1. Williams and Bors, *Growing Fruit in Northern Gardens*, 46–51; Poizner, "The Ultimate Guide to Fruit Tree Mulch," Orchard People (website); University of Massachusetts (website), "Mulching Tree Fruit and Small Fruit."

2. Gould, "Our Guide to Growing Strawberries: Plant Care Tips," Treehugger (website); Strik et al., "Growing Strawberries in Your Home Garden," Oregon State University (website).

3. Orange Pippin Fruit Trees (website), "Watering Your Fruit Trees"; MacArthur, "Watering Fruit Trees: When to Do It, and When to Avoid It," Food Gardening Network (website); Life Slice (website), "Fruit Tree Watering Requirements."

4. Poizner, *Growing Urban Orchards*, 58–62.

5. Poizner, *Growing Urban Orchards*, 38–39.

6. Williams and Bors, *Growing Fruit in Northern Gardens*, 260, 281–83.

7. Taylor, "12 Climbing Fruit Plants," Urban Garden Gal (website).

8. Jauron, "Training and Trellising Raspberries," Iowa State University (website).

9. Montana State University (website), "Choosing a Trellising System."

10. Penn State Extension (website), "Hardy Kiwi in the Home Fruit Planting."

11. The Daily Garden (website), "Suckers."

12. Buckner, "How to Prepare Fruit Trees for Winter," Gardener's Path (website); Poizner, "Five Easy Ways to Prepare Your Fruit Trees for Winter," Orchard People (website).

13. Williams and Bors, *Growing Fruit in Northern Gardens*, 278–80; Tilley, "Overwintering Grapes: How to Prepare Grapevines for Winter," Gardening Know How (website); Alberta Home Gardening (website), "How to Keep Your Grapevines Alive through the Winter."

14. Laidback Gardener (website), "The Fruit That Came in from the Cold."

Chapter Three

1. B. Grant, "Fruit Tree Pruning: How and When to Prune Fruit Trees," Gardening Know How (website); Poizner, "When to Prune Fruit Trees," Orchard People (website); Government of Ontario (website), "Pruning Fruit Trees."

2. University of Saskatchewan (website), "Sour Cherries."

3. Larum, "Spur Bearing Apple Info: Pruning Spur Bearing Apple Trees in the Landscape," Gardening Know How (website); Young, "How to Tell Tip-Bearing Apple Trees from Spur-Bearing Apple Trees," Garden Guides (website); United States Department of Agriculture Institute of Food and Agriculture (website), "What Are Fruiting Spurs on Apple Trees and Why Do Some Cultivars Have More Than Others?"

4. Ellis, *How to Prune Trees and Shrubs: Easy Techniques for Timely Trimming*, 21–23.

5. Ellis, *How to Prune Trees and Shrubs: Easy Techniques for Timely Trimming*, 14–20.

6. Fuller, "How to Espalier a Tree," *The Gardener for the Prairies*, 37; Stark Bro's (website), "How to Espalier Fruit Trees."

7. Deardorff and Wadsworth, *What's Wrong with My Fruit Garden?*, 270.

8. Government of Ontario (website), "Raspberries and Blackberries for Home Gardens."

9. Williams and Bors, *Growing Fruit in Northern Gardens*, 260; Jauron, "Pruning Raspberries in Late Winter/Early Spring," Iowa State University (website).

Chapter Four

1. Lundy, *Heritage Apples*, 4; Iowa State University (website), "Can I Grow an Apple Tree from Seed?"

2. Hollobone, *Propagation Techniques*, 96–97; Evans and Blazich, "Plant Propagation by Layering," North Carolina State Extension (website); Tilley, "Growing Strawberry Runners: What to Do with Strawberry Runners?," Gardening Know How (website).

3. Alberta Urban Garden (website), "Fruit Tree Grafting for Beginners"; Stephens, "Step-by-Step Guide to Grafting Fruit Trees," Mossy Oak (website).

4. Smith, *The Plant Propagator's Bible*, 78–79; Jauron, "Propagation of Shrubs from Softwood Cuttings," Iowa State University (website); Evans and Blazich, "Plant Propagation by Stem Cuttings," North Carolina State Extension (website).

Chapter Five

1. Williams and Bors, *Growing Fruit in Northern Gardens*, 90; Government of Manitoba (website), "Saskatoon Bud Moth (*Epinotia bicordana*)"; Government of Ontario (website), "Notes on Saskatoon Berry Insects: Saskatoon Bud Moth."

2. Ker and Walker, "Scale Insect Pests of Tree Fruit," Government of Ontario (website); BC Tree Fruit Production Guide (website), "San Jose Scale."

3. Natural Resources Canada (website), "Pear Sawfly (Pear Slug)"; Pellitteri, "Pear Slug (Pear Sawfly)," Wisconsin Horticulture (website); Iowa State University (website), "Pear Sawfly or Pearslug."

4. Messina and Smith, "Western Cherry Fruit Fly," Washington State University (website); Government of Canada (website), "*Rhagoletis cerasi* Eastern Cherry Fruit Fly Fact Sheet."

5. Government of British Columbia (website), "Spotted Wing Drosophila (Fruit Fly) Pest Alert"; Mintenko, "Spotted Wing Drosophila (*Drosophila suzukii*)," Government of Manitoba (website).

6. Government of Manitoba (website), "Chokecherry Gall Midge (*Contarinia virginianae*)."

7. Grabowski, "Leaf Spot Diseases of Trees and Shrubs," University of Minnesota Extension (website); Missouri Botanical Garden (website), "Leaf Spot Diseases of Shade Trees and Ornamentals."

8. Williams and Bors, *Growing Fruit in Northern Gardens*, 99.

9. Deardorff and Wadsworth, *What's Wrong with My Fruit Garden?*, 208; Government of Ontario (website), "Apple Scab"; Toronto Master Gardeners (website), "Crabapple Tree with Apple Scab."

10. Government of Ontario (website), "White Pine Blister Rust."

11. Government of British Columbia (website), "White Pine Blister Rust."

12. Williams and Bors, *Growing Fruit in Northern Gardens*, 181–90; Michigan Department of Agriculture and Rural Development (website), "White Pine Blister Rust Resistant Currant and Gooseberry Varieties."

13. Carroll, "Verticillium Wilt Treatment: What Is Verticillium Wilt and How to Fix It," Gardening Know How (website); Missouri Botanical Garden (website), "Verticillium Wilt."

14. University of Illinois Extension (website), "Virus Diseases of Brambles in the Midwest."

15. Williams and Bors, *Growing Fruit in Northern Gardens*, 110–11; Cornell University (website), "Raspberries: Leaves Are Curled, Rolled or Crinkled"; Government of Ontario (website), "Notes on Raspberry Diseases: Viruses."

16. White, "Why Wasps Become So Annoying at the End of Summer," The Conversation (website).

17. A. Grant, "Do Fruit Trees Attract Wasps: Tips on Keeping Wasps Away from Fruit Trees," Gardening Know How (website); *Gardeners' World* (website), "Wasp Damage on Apples and Pears."

18. Ralph, *Grow a Little Fruit Tree*, 137–38; Williams and Bors, *Growing Fruit in Northern Gardens*, 118; The Practical Planter (website), "10 Smart Ways to Keep Birds Away from Fruit Trees."

19. Poizner, *Growing Urban Orchards*, 45–46.

20. Hoover, "How Rootstocks Influence Apple Trees," *Fruit Growers News* (website); Jauron, "Why Isn't My Apple Tree Bearing Fruit?," Iowa State University (website).

21. Patterson, "Apple Tree Problems: How to Get Fruit on Apple Trees," Gardening Know How (website).

22. Williams and Bors, *Growing Fruit in Northern Gardens*, 24.

23. Iowa State University (website), "The Flesh Near the Centers of My Apples Has a Glassy Appearance. Why?"

24. A. Grant, "Fruit Split in Cherries: Learn Why Cherry Fruit Splits Open," Gardening Know How (website); Lang, "Stone Fruit: Avoiding Cherry Fruit Cracking Is a Balancing Act," Growing Produce (website).

25. Consumer Reports (website), "Q&A: Is the Cloudy Coating on Blueberries Safe to Eat?"

26. Longstroth, "How Should Fruit Growers Respond to Hail and Severe Storms?," Michigan State University Extension (website).

Chapter Six

1. The Urban Farmer (website), "Edible Plants for the Prairies"; Northern Bushcraft (website), "Edible Berries of Alberta"; Northern Bushcraft (website), "Edible Berries of Saskatchewan"; Northern Bushcraft (website), "Edible Berries of Manitoba."

2. Proctor, "Fruit Cultivation," The Canadian Encyclopedia (website); Hanson, "Unusual Fruit Plants for Gardens in the North Central Region," Michigan State University Extension (website); Garden Therapy (website), "Unique Edible Fruit Plants You Need to Grow in Your Garden"; Demchak, "Goji Berry Culture," PennState Extension (website); Allotment and Gardens (website), "Growing Tayberries—How to Grow Tayberries"; Native Plants PNW (website), "Red Huckleberry, *Vaccinium parvifolium*."

3. Sproule, "Growing Watermelon from Seed," Salisbury Greenhouse (website); Wildrose Heritage Seed Company (website), "Watermelon—Cream of Saskatchewan."

4. The Canadian Organic Grower (website), "Ground Cherries."

5. Iowa State University (website), "What Are the Differences between the Different Types of Strawberries?"; University of Saskatchewan (website), "Strawberries."

6. Williams and Bors, *Growing Fruit in Northern Gardens*, 159–64.

7. The Urban Farmer (website), "Edible Plants for the Prairies"; Northern Bushcraft (website), "Blueberry."

8. Williams and Bors, *Growing Fruit in Northern Gardens*, 178; Smith, "Why the Tomato Was Feared in Europe for More Than 200 Years," *Smithsonian Magazine* (website); Ontario Poison Centre (website), "Fruit Pits."

9. Radula-Scott, *Storing Home Grown Fruit & Veg*, 68–74, 118–20, 127–29, 137–42, 159–64, 168–72, 179–82; HGTV (website), "When to Harvest Pumpkins"; Iowa State University (website), "How Do I Know When a Watermelon Is Ready to Harvest?"

10. University of Nebraska–Lincoln (website), "Fruits That Continue to Ripen After Picking"; Porter, "Ripe for the Picking—Which Fruits Keep Ripening After Harvest?," The Garden Professors (website).

Sources

Alberta Home Gardening. "How to Keep Your Grapevines Alive through the Winter." January 18, 2008. albertahomegardening.com/how-to-keep-your -grapevines-alive-through-the-winter/.

Alberta Urban Garden. "Fruit Tree Grafting for Beginners." April 29, 2016. albertaurbangarden.ca/2016/04/29/fruit-tree-grafting-for-beginners/.

Allotment and Gardens. "Growing Tayberries—How to Grow Tayberries." Accessed April 4, 2022. allotment-garden.org/fruit/tayberries-growing/.

Armstrong, W.P. "Identification of Major Fruit Types." Accessed April 1, 2022. palomar.edu/users/warmstrong/fruitid1.htm.

BC Tree Fruit Production Guide. "San Jose Scale." Accessed April 3, 2022. bctfpg .ca/pest_guide/info/57/.

BioAdvanced. "Growing Trees: Bare-Root Advantages and Timing." Accessed April 1, 2022. bioadvanced.com/growing-trees-bare-root-advantages-and-timing/.

Britannica. "Fruit." Last updated March 28, 2022. britannica.com/science/fruit -plant-reproductive-body.

Brown, Diane, and Duke Elsner. "Considerations for Growing Backyard Tree Fruit." Michigan State University. canr.msu.edu/news/considerations_for_growing _backyard_tree_fruit.

Buckner, Heather. "How to Prepare Fruit Trees for Winter." Gardener's Path. November 13, 2020. gardenerspath.com/plants/fruit-trees/winterize/.

Byrne, Mary K., and Dr. Victoria Wojcik. "Selecting Plants for Pollinators." Pollinator Partnership Canada. Accessed April 1, 2022. pollinator.org/PDFs/Guides /LowerMainland.ver6.hires.pdf.

The Canadian Organic Grower. "Ground Cherries." April 1, 2011. magazine.cog .ca/article/ground-cherries/.

Carroll, Jackie. "Verticillium Wilt Treatment: What Is Verticillium Wilt and How to Fix It." Gardening Know How. gardeningknowhow.com/plant-problems/disease /verticillium-wilt-treatment.htm.

Cloud Mountain Farm Center. "Encouraging Pollinators in Your Orchard and Garden." Accessed April 1, 2022. cloudmountainfarmcenter.org/education/grow -tips/encouraging-pollinators-in-your-orchard/.

Consumer Reports. "Q&A: Is the Cloudy Coating on Blueberries Safe to Eat?" May 17, 2010. consumerreports.org/cro/news/2010/05/q-a-is-the-cloudy-coating-on -blueberries-safe-to-eat/index.htm.

Cornell University. "Raspberries: Leaves Are Curled, Rolled or Crinkled." Accessed April 4, 2022. blogs.cornell.edu/berrytool/raspberries/raspberries-leaves-are-curled -rolled-or-crinkled/.

The Daily Garden. "Suckers." March 4, 2016. thedailygarden.us/garden-word-of
-the-day/suckers.

Deardorff, David, and Kathryn Wadsworth. *What's Wrong with My Fruit Garden?*
Portland, OR: Timber Press, 2013.

Deep Green Permaculture. "Backyard Orchard Culture, a New Approach to
Growing Fruit in Limited Spaces." Accessed April 1, 2022. deepgreenpermaculture
.com/2010/01/01/backyard-orchard-culture/.

Demchak, Kathy. "Goji Berry Culture." PennState Extension. Last updated
October 26, 2016. extension.psu.edu/goji-berry-culture.

Ellis, Barbara. *How to Prune Trees and Shrubs: Easy Techniques for Timely
Trimming.* North Adams, MA: Storey Publishing, 2016.

Epic Gardening. "Raspberry Raised Bed Tips: Getting Things Growing." Last
updated December 4, 2020. epicgardening.com/raspberry-raised-bed/.

Evans, Ervin, and Frank Blazich. "Plant Propagation by Layering." North Carolina
State Extension. January 31, 1999. content.ces.ncsu.edu/plant-propagation-by
-layering-instructions-for-the-home-gardener.

———. "Plant Propagation by Stem Cuttings." North Carolina State Extension.
January 31, 1999. content.ces.ncsu.edu/plant-propagation-by-stem-cuttings
-instructions-for-the-home-gardener.

Fuller, Lauren. "How to Espalier a Tree." *The Gardener for the Prairies,* Winter 2005.

Gardener's Supply Company. "Growing Berries and Asparagus in Raised Beds." Last
updated February 25, 2021. gardeners.com/how-to/berries-asparagus-raised-beds/7562.html.

Gardeners' World. "Wasp Damage on Apples and Pears." March 6, 2019.
gardenersworld.com/how-to/solve-problems/wasp-damage-on-apples-and-pears/.

Garden Therapy. "Unique Edible Fruit Plants You Need to Grow in Your Garden."
Accessed April 4, 2022. gardentherapy.ca/unique-edible-fruit-plants/.

Gould, Kerin. "Our Guide to Growing Strawberries: Plant Care Tips." Treehugger. July
22, 2021. treehugger.com/our-guide-to-growing-strawberries-plant-care-tips-5192816.

Government of British Columbia. "Spotted Wing Drosophila (Fruit Fly) Pest
Alert." Accessed April 3, 2022. gov.bc.ca/gov/content/industry/agriculture-seafood
/animals-and-crops/plant-health/insects-and-plant-diseases/tree-fruits/spotted-wing
-drosophila.

———. "White Pine Blister Rust." Accessed April 4, 2022. gov.bc.ca/gov/content
/industry/forestry/managing-our-forest-resources/forest-health/invasive-forest
-pests/white-pine-blister-rust.

Government of Canada. "*Rhagoletis cerasi* Eastern Cherry Fruit Fly Fact Sheet."
Last updated July 2, 2019. inspection.canada.ca/plant-health/invasive-species/insects
/european-cherry-fruit-fly/fact-sheet/eng/1467913088353/1467914654510.

Government of Manitoba. "Chokecherry Gall Midge (*Contarinia
virginianae*)." Accessed April 3, 2022. gov.mb.ca/agriculture/crops/insects
/print,chokecherry-gall-midge.html.

———. "Saskatoon Bud Moth (*Epinotia bicordana*)." Accessed April 3, 2022. gov.mb.ca/agriculture/crops/insects/saskatoon-bud-moth.html.

Government of Ontario. "Apple Scab." Accessed April 4, 2022. omafra.gov.on.ca /english/crops/facts/apscab.htm.

———. "Notes on Raspberry Diseases: Viruses." Last updated February 12, 2021. omafra.gov.on.ca/english/crops/pub360/notes/raspvirus.htm.

———. "Notes on Saskatoon Berry Insects: Saskatoon Bud Moth." Last updated February 12, 2021. omafra.gov.on.ca/english/crops/pub360/notes/saskbmoth.htm.

———. "Pruning Fruit Trees." Last updated February 12, 2021. omafra.gov.on.ca /english/crops/facts/00-005.htm.

———. "Raspberries and Blackberries for Home Gardens." February 12, 2021. omafra.gov.on.ca/english/crops/facts/99-033.htm.

———. "White Pine Blister Rust." Last updated May 20, 2021. ontario.ca/page /white-pine-blister-rust.

Grabowski, Michelle. "Leaf Spot Diseases of Trees and Shrubs." University of Minnesota Extension. Last updated 2018. extension.umn.edu/plant-diseases/leaf -spot-diseases-trees-and-shrubs.

Grant, Amy. "Do Fruit Trees Attract Wasps: Tips on Keeping Wasps Away from Fruit Trees." Gardening Know How. Last updated March 22, 2022. gardeningknowhow.com/edible/fruits/fegen/wasps-in-fruit-trees.htm.

———. "Fruit Bearing Shade Plants: Growing Fruiting Plants for Shade Gardens." Gardening Know How. Last updated March 22, 2022. gardeningknowhow.com /edible/fruits/fegen/fruit-bearing-shade-plants.htm.

———. "Fruit Split in Cherries: Learn Why Cherry Fruit Splits Open." Gardening Know How. Last updated May 2, 2014. gardeningknowhow.com/edible /fruits/cherry/fruit-split-in-cherries.htm.

———. "Understanding Different Fruit Types." Gardening Know How. Last updated March 22, 2022. gardeningknowhow.com/edible/fruits/fegen/different-fruit-types.htm.

Grant, Bonnie L. "Fruit Tree Pruning: How and When to Prune Fruit Trees." Gardening Know How. gardeningknowhow.com/edible/fruits/fegen/fruit-tree -pruning.htm.

Hanson, Eric. "Unusual Fruit Plants for Gardens in the North Central Region." Michigan State University Extension. October 26, 2015. canr.msu.edu/resources /unusual_fruit_plants_for_gardens_in_the_north_central_region_e2747.

Harvey, Ailsa. "What's the Difference between Fruit and Vegetables?" Live Science. January 26, 2022. livescience.com/33991-difference-fruits-vegetables.html.

HGTV. "When to Harvest Pumpkins." Accessed April 4, 2022. hgtv.com/outdoors /flowers-and-plants/vegetables/when-to-harvest-pumpkins.

Hollobone, Julie. *Propagation Techniques*. London, UK: New Holland Publishers, 2008.

Hoover, Emily E. "How Rootstocks Influence Apple Trees." *Fruit Growers News*. November 7, 2018. fruitgrowersnews.com/news/how-rootstocks-influence-apple-trees/.

Huffstetler, Erin. "Fruits That Grow in the Shade." The Spruce. Last updated March 1, 2021. thespruce.com/fruits-that-grow-in-the-shade-1388680.

Iowa State University. "Can I Grow an Apple Tree from Seed?" Accessed April 3, 2022. https://hortnews.extension.iastate.edu/faq/can-i-grow-apple-tree-seed.

———. "The Flesh Near the Centers of My Apples Has a Glassy Appearance. Why?" Accessed April 4, 2022. hortnews.extension.iastate.edu/faq/flesh-near -centers-my-apples-has-glassy-appearance-why.

———. "How Do I Know When a Watermelon Is Ready to Harvest?" Accessed April 4, 2022. hortnews.extension.iastate.edu/faq/how-do-i-know-when-watermelon-ready-harvest.

———. "Pear Sawfly or Pearslug." Accessed April 3, 2022. hortnews.extension .iastate.edu/pear-sawfly-or-pearslug.

———. "What Are the Differences between the Different Types of Strawberries?" Accessed April 4, 2022. hortnews.extension.iastate.edu/faq/what-are-differences -between-different-types-strawberries.

Jauron, Richard. "Propagation of Shrubs from Softwood Cuttings." Iowa State University. June 6, 2003. hortnews.extension.iastate.edu/2003/6-6-2003/softwood.html.

———. "Pruning Raspberries in Late Winter/Early Spring." Iowa State University. February 9, 2011. hortnews.extension.iastate.edu/2011/2-9/raspberries.html.

———. "Training and Trellising Raspberries." Iowa State University. May 7, 2008. hortnews.extension.iastate.edu/2008/5-7/raspberry.html.

———. "Why Isn't My Apple Tree Bearing Fruit?" Iowa State University. Accessed April 4, 2022. hortnews.extension.iastate.edu/faq/why-isn%E2 %80%99t-my-apple-tree-bearing-fruit.

Kelly, Lawrence M. "What Is a Fruit?" New York Botanical Garden. August 6, 2014. nybg.org/blogs/science-talk/2014/08/what-is-a-fruit/.

Ker, Kevin W., and Gerald M. Walker. "Scale Insect Pests of Tree Fruit." Government of Ontario. Last updated February 12, 2021. omafra.gov.on.ca/english /crops/facts/90-120.htm.

Kington, Miles. "Miles Kington Quotes." Goodreads. Accessed June 11, 2022. goodreads.com/author/quotes/164685.Miles_Kington.

Laidback Gardener. "The Fruit That Came in from the Cold." May 10, 2017. laidbackgardener.blog/2017/05/10/the-fruit-that-came-in-from-the-cold/.

Lang, Gregory. "Stone Fruit: Avoiding Cherry Fruit Cracking Is a Balancing Act." Growing Produce. May 2, 2014. growingproduce.com/fruits/stone-fruit-avoiding -cherry-fruit-cracking-is-a-balancing-act/.

Larum, Darcy. "Spur Bearing Apple Info: Pruning Spur Bearing Apple Trees in the Landscape." Gardening Know How. March 22, 2022. gardeningknowhow.com/edible /fruits/apples/spur-bearing-apple-trees.htm.

Life Slice. "Fruit Tree Watering Requirements." Accessed April 1, 2022. life-slice .com/fruit-tree-water-requirements.html.

Longstroth, Mark. "How Should Fruit Growers Respond to Hail and Severe Storms?" Michigan State University Extension. July 12, 2016. canr.msu.edu/news /how_should_fruit_growers_respond_to_hail_and_severe_storms.

Lundy, Susan. *Heritage Apples*. Victoria: TouchWood Editions, 2013.

MacArthur, Amanda. "Watering Fruit Trees: When to Do It, and When to Avoid It." Food Gardening Network. January 13, 2022. foodgardening.mequoda.com/daily /watering-irrigation/watering-fruit-trees-when-to-do-it-and-when-to-avoid-it/.

McGinnis, Esther E. "Smart Gardening: Pollination in Vegetable Gardens and Backyard Fruit." Michigan State University. October 1, 2018. canr.msu.edu /resources/smart-gardening-pollination-in-vegetable-gardens-and-backyard-fruit.

Messina, Frank J., and Timothy J. Smith. "Western Cherry Fruit Fly." Washington State University. Last updated August 2010. treefruit.wsu.edu/crop-protection/opm /western-cherry-fruit-fly/.

Michigan Department of Agriculture and Rural Development. "White Pine Blister Rust Resistant Currant and Gooseberry Varieties." Last updated January 19, 2022. michigan.gov/-/media/Project/Websites/mdard/documents/pesticide-plant-pest /planthealth/white_pine_blister_rust_resistant_currant_and_gooseberry_varieties.pdf.

Mintenko, Anthony. "Spotted Wing Drosophila (*Drosophila suzukii*)." Government of Manitoba. Last updated June 22, 2021. gov.mb.ca/agriculture/crops/insects /spotted-winged-drosophila.html.

Missouri Botanical Garden. "Leaf Spot Diseases of Shade Trees and Ornamentals." Accessed April 4, 2022. missouribotanicalgarden.org/gardens-gardening/your -garden/help-for-the-home-gardener/advice-tips-resources/pests-and-problems /diseases/fungal-spots/leaf-spot-shade.aspx.

———. "Verticillium Wilt." Accessed April 4, 2022. missouribotanicalgarden.org /gardens-gardening/your-garden/help-for-the-home-gardener/advice-tips -resources/pests-and-problems/diseases/cankers/verticillium-wilt.aspx

Montana State University. "Choosing a Trellising System." Accessed April 2, 2022. agresearch.montana.edu/warc/guides/grapes/establishing-new-vineyard/trellising.html.

Native Plants PNW. "Red Huckleberry, *Vaccinium parvifolium*." February 8, 2016. nativeplantspnw.com/red-huckleberry-vaccinium-parvifolium/.

Natural Resources Canada. "Pear Sawfly (Pear Slug)." August 4, 2015. tidcf.nrcan .gc.ca/en/insects/factsheet/7688.

Northern Bushcraft. "Blueberry." Accessed April 4, 2022. northernbushcraft.com /topic.php?name=blueberry&region=ab&ctgy=edible_berries.

———. "Edible Berries of Alberta." Accessed April 4, 2022. northernbushcraft .com/guide.php?ctgy=edible_berries&region=ab.

———. "Edible Berries of Manitoba." Accessed April 4, 2022. northernbushcraft .com/guide.php?ctgy=edible_berries&region=mb.

———. "Edible Berries of Saskatchewan." Accessed April 4, 2022. northernbushcraft.com/guide.php?ctgy=edible_berries&region=sk.

Ontario Poison Centre. "Fruit Pits." Accessed April 4, 2022. ontariopoisoncentre.ca /household-hazards-items/fruit-pits/.

Orange Pippin Fruit Trees. "Watering Your Fruit Trees." Accessed April 1, 2022. orangepippintrees.com/articles/planting-growing/watering-fruit-trees.

Patterson, Susan. "Apple Tree Problems: How to Get Fruit on Apple Trees." Gardening Know How. Last updated March 22, 2022. gardeningknowhow.com /edible/fruits/apples/no-fruit-on-apple-trees.htm.

Pellitteri, Phil. "Pear Slug (Pear Sawfly)." Wisconsin Horticulture. Accessed April 3, 2022. hort.extension.wisc.edu/articles/pear-slug-pear-sawfly/.

Penn State Extension. "Hardy Kiwi in the Home Fruit Planting." Last updated August 9, 2016. extension.psu.edu/hardy-kiwi-in-the-home-fruit-planting.

Poizner, Susan. "Five Easy Ways to Prepare Your Fruit Trees for Winter." Orchard People. November 24, 2021. orchardpeople.com/how-to-prepare-fruit-trees-for-winter/.

———. *Growing Urban Orchards*. Toronto: Orchard People, 2017.

———. "The Ultimate Guide to Fruit Tree Mulch." Orchard People. June 7, 2021. https://orchardpeople.com/fruit-tree-mulch/.

———. "When to Prune Fruit Trees." Orchard People. August 4, 2021. orchardpeople.com/when-to-prune-fruit-trees/.

———. "Why Buy a Young Whip If There Are Large Fruit Trees for Sale?" Orchard People. May 14, 2021. orchardpeople.com/whats-betterplanting-a-young -fruit-tree-whip-or-an-older-fruit-tree/.

Porter, John. "Ripe for the Picking—Which Fruits Keep Ripening After Harvest?" The Garden Professors. June 14, 2019. gardenprofessors.com/ripening/.

The Practical Planter. "10 Smart Ways to Keep Birds Away from Fruit Trees." Last updated October 1, 2021. thepracticalplanter.com/how-to-keep-birds-away-from -fruit-trees/.

Proctor, J.T.A. "Fruit Cultivation." The Canadian Encyclopedia. November 26, 2015. thecanadianencyclopedia.ca/en/article/fruit-cultivation.

Radula-Scott, Caroline. *Storing Home Grown Fruit & Veg*. London, UK: W. Foulsham, 2011.

Ralph, Ann. *Grow a Little Fruit Tree*. North Adams, MA: Storey Publishing, 2014.

Saleem, M. Imran. "How to Grow Blueberries in a Raised Bed?" Bed-Gardening. Accessed April 1, 2022. bedgardening.com/how-to-grow-blueberries-in-a-raised-bed/.

Smith, K. Annabelle. "Why the Tomato Was Feared in Europe for More Than 200 Years." *Smithsonian Magazine*. June 18, 2013. smithsonianmag.com/arts-culture /why-the-tomato-was-feared-in-europe-for-more-than-200-years-863735/.

Smith, Miranda. *The Plant Propagator's Bible*. New York: Reader's Digest Association, 2007.

Sproule, Rob. "Growing Watermelon from Seed." Salisbury Greenhouse. Accessed April 4, 2022. salisburygreenhouse.com/growing-watermelon-from-seed/.

Stark Bro's. "How to Espalier Fruit Trees." Accessed April 3, 2022. starkbros.com /growing-guide/article/espalier-fruit-trees.

Stephens, Jarrod E. "Step-by-Step Guide to Grafting Fruit Trees." Mossy Oak. November 14, 2019. mossyoak.com/our-obsession/blogs/how-to/step-by-step-guide -to-grafting-fruit-trees.

Strik, B., et al. "Growing Strawberries in Your Home Garden." Oregon State University. Last updated July 2020. catalog.extension.oregonstate.edu/sites/catalog /files/project/pdf/ec1307.pdf.

Taylor, Kelly. "12 Climbing Fruit Plants." Urban Garden Gal. Accessed April 1, 2022. urbangardengal.com/climbing-fruit-plants/.

Tilley, Nikki. "Growing Strawberry Runners: What to Do with Strawberry Runners?" Gardening Know How. Last updated March 22, 2022. gardeningknowhow.com/edible/fruits/strawberry/growing-strawberry-runners.htm.

———. "Overwintering Grapes: How to Prepare Grapevines for Winter." Gardening Know How. Last updated March 22, 2022. gardeningknowhow.com /edible/fruits/grapes/grape-vine-winter-care.htm.

Toronto Master Gardeners. "Crabapple Tree with Apple Scab." Accessed April 4, 2022. torontomastergardeners.ca/askagardener/crabapple-tree-with-apple-scab/.

United States Department of Agriculture Institute of Food and Agriculture. "What Are Fruiting Spurs on Apple Trees and Why Do Some Cultivars Have More Than Others?" August 22, 2019. apples.extension.org/what-are-fruiting-spurs-on-apple -trees-and-why-do-some-cultivars-have-more-than-others/.

University of Illinois Extension. "Virus Diseases of Brambles in the Midwest." November 1996. ipm.illinois.edu/diseases/rpds/710.pdf.

University of Massachusetts. "Mulching Tree Fruit and Small Fruit." Accessed April 1, 2022. ag.umass.edu/sites/ag.umass.edu/files/fact-sheets/pdf/mulching_fruit.pdf.

University of Nebraska–Lincoln. "Fruits That Continue to Ripen After Picking." Accessed April 4, 2022. food.unl.edu/article/fruits-continue-ripen-after-picking.

University of Saskatchewan. "Sour Cherries." Accessed April 3, 2022. gardening.usask.ca/gardening-advice/gardenline-nested-pages/food-plant-pages /fruit/sour-cherries.php.

———. "Strawberries." Accessed April 4, 2022. gardening.usask.ca/gardening -advice/gardenline-nested-pages/food-plant-pages/fruit/strawberry.php.

The Urban Farmer. "Edible Plants for the Prairies." Accessed April 4, 2022. theurbanfarmer.ca/edible-plants-for-the-prairies.

White, Scott. "Why Wasps Become So Annoying at the End of Summer." The Conversation. August 27, 2020. theconversation.com/why-wasps-become-so -annoying-at-the-end-of-summer-145053.

Wildrose Heritage Seed Company. "Watermelon—Cream of Saskatchewan." Accessed April 4, 2022. wildroseheritageseed.com/store/p180/Watermelon _-_Cream_of_Saskatchewan.html.

Williams, Sara, and Bob Bors. *Growing Fruit in Northern Gardens*. Regina: Coteau Books, 2017.

Young, James. "How to Tell Tip-Bearing Apple Trees from Spur-Bearing Apple Trees." Garden Guides. September 21, 2017. gardenguides.com/98724-tell-tip -bearing-apple-trees-spur-bearing-apple-trees.html.

Index

Page numbers in italics refer to photographs.

NOTES

NOTES

© *Steve Melrose*

About the Authors

SHERYL NORMANDEAU was born and raised in the Peace Country region of northern Alberta and has made Calgary her home since 1994. A writer and master gardener, Sheryl holds a bachelor's degree in English as well as a Prairie Horticulture Certificate and an Urban Sustainable Agriculture Certificate. Since 2013, she has served as the online Ask an Expert for the Calgary Horticultural Society. She works at the Calgary Public Library—besides gardening, books of all kinds are her grand passion! She is a small-space gardener (on a tiny balcony and in a plot in a nearby community garden) and she is most enthusiastic about growing veggies. She lives with her husband, Rob, and their rescue cat Smudge. Find Sheryl at Flowery Prose (floweryprose.com) and on Facebook (@FloweryProse), Twitter (@Flowery_Prose), and Instagram (flowery_prose).

JANET MELROSE was born in Trinidad, West Indies, and immigrated to Canada in 1964. She has lived in Calgary since 1969. She is a master gardener and the creator and owner of the successful horticulture business Calgary's Cottage Gardener, which specializes in garden education and consultation, horticultural therapy, and advocating for sustainable local food systems. She holds bachelor's degrees in sociology and history, a Prairie Horticulture Certificate, and a Horticultural Therapy Certificate. Janet is a lifelong gardener, coming from a heritage of English gardening. She has a large garden at home in the suburbs of Calgary that can only be described as a typical cottage garden. She cares for eight other gardens throughout Calgary through her work as a horticultural therapist as well as a bed at the Inglewood Community Garden. She is married to Steve and has two children, Jennifer and David. Three cats, Patrick, Theo, and Mia, currently own their home and patrol against the deer, hares, squirrels, skunk, mice, insects, and assorted birds that believe the garden is theirs, too! Connect with Janet on Facebook (@Calgarys-Cottage-Gardener), Twitter (@CalCottageGrdnr), and Instagram (CalgarysCottageGardener).

About the Series

It looks like you've discovered the Guides for the Prairie Gardener! This budding series puts the combined knowledge of two lifelong prairie gardeners at your grubby fingertips. Whether you've just cleared a few square feet for your first bed of veggies or are a seasoned green thumb stumped by that one cultivar you can't seem to master, we think you'll find Janet and Sheryl the ideal teachers. Find answers on seeds, soil, trees, flowers, weather, climate, pests, pots, and quite a few more. These slim but mighty volumes, handsomely designed, make great companions at the height of summer in the garden trenches and during cold winter days planning the next season. With regional expertise, elegance, and a sense of humour, Janet and Sheryl take your questions and turn them into prairie gardening inspiration. For more information, and for other titles in the series, visit touchwoodeditions.com/guidesprairiegardener.